MENTAL DISORDER

MENTAL DISORDER

Nichola Khan

ANTHROPOLOGICAL INSIGHTS

UNIVERSITY OF TORONTO PRESS

www.utppublishing.com

Library and Archives Canada Cataloguing in Publication

Khan, Nichola, author
    Mental disorder / Nichola Khan.

(Anthropological insights)
Includes bibliographical references and index.
Issued in print and electronic formats.
ISBN 978-1-4426-3534-0 (hardback).—ISBN 978-1-4426-3533-3 (paperback).
—ISBN 978-1-4426-3535-7 (html).—ISBN 978-1-4426-3536-4 (pdf).

    1. Mental illness–Cross-cultural studies. 2. Mental illness–Social aspects.
3. Cultural psychiatry. 4. Ethnopsychology. 5. Medical anthropology. I. Title.
II. Series: Anthropological insights.

RC455.4.E8K53 2017   362.196'890089   C2016-903411-9
                                                     C2016-903412-7

We welcome comments and suggestions regarding any aspect of our publications—please feel free to contact us at news@utphighereducation.com or visit our Internet site at www.utppublishing.com.

North America
5201 Dufferin Street
North York, Ontario, Canada, M3H 5T8

2250 Military Road
Tonawanda, New York, USA, 14150

ORDERS PHONE: 1-800-565-9523
ORDERS FAX: 1-800-221-9985
ORDERS E-MAIL: utpbooks@utpress.utoronto.ca

UK, Ireland, and continental Europe
NBN International
Estover Road, Plymouth, PL6 7PY, UK

ORDERS PHONE: 44 (0) 1752 202301
ORDERS FAX: 44 (0) 1752 202333
ORDERS E-MAIL: enquiries@
nbninternational.com

Every effort has been made to contact copyright holders; in the event of an error or omission, please notify the publisher.

The University of Toronto Press acknowledges the financial support for its publishing activities of the Government of Canada through the Canada Book Fund.

Printed in the United States of America.
Cover design: Grace Cheong.

A Soul hung up, as t'were, in Chains Of Nerves, and Arteries, and Veins. Tortur'd, besides each other part,

In a vain Head, and double Heart.

From "A Dialogue Between the Soul and Body" by
Andrew Marvell (1681)

CONTENTS

PREFACE

This short book introduces anthropological insights into mental disorder.
It reflects a growing interest in anthropology's encounter with the key
"psych" disciplines and the human and social sciences. This is evident in
the well-spring of new university courses in psychological and psychiatric
anthropology in the United States, Canada, and Australia, and the transnational migration of this interest to Europe, Asia, and the global South.
It also continues the story of the ways "madness" has been understood over
the past two centuries. This involves ways divisions have been established,
monitored, and protected by professionals who have claimed authority
over their particular specialty to illuminate the mind's darkness, and variously defined themselves as psychiatrists, psychoanalysts, anthropologists,
psychologists, criminologists, psycho-pharmacologists, and neuroscientists.
Their treatments have included electroshock therapy, hypnosis, leucotomy,
bloodletting, coma, banishment, confinement, pharmaceuticals, talking,
filming, and writing. The challenge for this book thus lies in synthesiz-
ing some diverse literatures in a concise, engaging, and accessible way for
undergraduate and graduate students, clinician practitioners, specialists,
and the simply curious.

In doing so, it highlights continuities and also departures from anthropology's traditional purview of shamanism, ritual and religious healing,
traditional medicine, and spirit possession. It also departs from earlier
forays into psychological anthropology. Several older readers in psychological anthropology draw heavily on psychological theory and applications
across diverse topics not necessarily related to mental health—hence the
focus being "too general." In engaging mental health and illness, others
tended to prioritize the lens of culture, or else single disorders—hence
the focus, although rich, "too narrow." This book represents an attempt to
bridge the lacuna. Its aim—avoiding both uncritical presentism and rigid
historicization—is to track ways anthropologists have widened their thinking about madness through conversations with not only "psy-entists" but
also epidemiologists, addiction and legal experts, journalists, filmmakers,
activists, patients, and sufferers. Given the proliferation of research on the
brain and psyche in anthropology, and in this field more broadly, the book's
cartography is inevitably partial. The end-of-chapter sections containing

further readings, ethnographic films, blogs, websites, and activities are suggested as valuable tools for cutting through the complexity of the literature. They are designed to provoke useful reflection, rather than to meet specific learning outcomes, and to encourage further investigation. The hope is readers will use these sources as a guide and make their own additions.

No one is immune to mental illness. If most of us are sane, we are only relatively so. Madness is ever near. This topic concerns human suffering. Mental disorders affect people who research, teach, and also study them. Students may be drawn to this topic because they or someone they know have suffered from diagnosed or undiagnosed mental disorders. If this applies to you, you are advised to take care while engaging with the topics in this book, and to seek out available avenues of support from your institutions and communities if you need to.

Mental disorder is no longer overwhelmingly perceived in terms of threat, danger, and radical difference. Statistics show that many of us will be affected during our lifetimes. The mythical image of the violent psychopath (never included as a discrete disorder in either of the world's largest two psychiatric classification manuals) has been largely relegated to the fearsome imagery of drama, films, and literature. While such behavior exists, and may be organically distinctive, the key point to stress is that "madness" exists on a continuum. The World Health Organization is updating its data on global rates of mental illness. It estimates around 450 million people worldwide suffer from a mental disorder—the most common being anxiety disorders, followed by mood disorders (including major depression) and substance abuse. The incidence of personality disorders may be as high as 15 per cent, and an estimated 26 million people suffer from schizophrenia worldwide. These figures are, moreover, seen as underestimated due to poor diagnosis and low reporting rates. Recalling Winston Churchill's maxim, "Lies, damn lies, and statistics," we might additionally question if they reflect a higher prevalence of mental illness that is related to global, modern living conditions or perhaps better ways of capturing what was always there. Does the medicalization of unhappiness invite new drugs, which, in turn, invite mirror illnesses? Does the emergence of new disorders and diagnoses signify new ways of interpreting peoples' inability to cope? This book offers a toolkit for subjecting many such questions to investigation. For a long time I have felt marginal in two disciplines largely hostile to each other (an anthropologist often at large in psychology, a psychologist abroad in anthropology). It is therefore very heartening to me, and increasing numbers of others like me, that the purchase of disciplinary claims to splendid isolation is fast becoming wholly untenable.

I gratefully acknowledge the support of the School of Applied Social Science at the University of Brighton, my colleagues, and my final-year students who have allowed me to teach the material in this book as a course entitled "Mental Disorder and Anthropology." I am grateful to John Barker at the University of Toronto Press, Higher Education Division for taking on the project, and to my wonderful editor, Anne Brackenbury, for encouraging and persuading it, and me, to fruition with such generous good cheer. Likewise, I thank S. and S. for their good humor and forbearance in coping with the extreme moods, obsessive behavior, and distractedness that shape life with a working mother who has a book in progress. I hope these skills will stand them well in life.

Lives dominated, interrupted, or ruptured by madness can be painful and terrible, but also productive and joyful. In my own moments of insanity, I have been restored not necessarily to sanity (a happily shifting signifier) but to equilibrium and "life" by tenuous and tenacious attachments to ideas, places, occasional therapies, and medicines, and to those people who accompanied me through terrors and back again. This book is dedicated to them.

INTRODUCTION

This book introduces ways anthropologists from different traditions approach mental disorder, treatment, and recovery. The topic relates to anthropology's wider engagements with cultural psychiatry, politics, psychoanalysis, medicine, law, human rights, and global mental health. The book also clarifies some intellectual shifts from a biological focus on race in the first half of the twentieth century, to an emphasis on culture that dominated largely until the 1980s, to an interest after the 1990s in ways mental disorder is shaped by institutional forms of power and globalization. These concerns subsequently gave way to a focus on the increasing medicalization of psychiatry by the pharmaceutical industry, and the return of biological explanations centered on genetics, neuroscience, and ideas of heredity. Bringing together this diverse array of applications, this book charts some conceptual frameworks, interpretations, and anthropological insights into mental disorder. These draw on anthropology's classic traditions of ethnography and long-term fieldwork and on questions concerning anthropology's relevance to a rapidly globalizing world. These transformations, we will see, are in part also driven by anthropology's struggles to overcome its own identity problems rooted in esotericism, elitism, and the legacy of colonialism.

Why mental disorder? First, psychiatry works with diagnostic manuals. The world's largest de facto system is *The Diagnostic and Statistical Manual of Mental Disorders* (DSM), published by the American Psychiatric Association, containing around 300 diagnoses. The DSM-5 was published in 2013. The DSM shares similarities with the *International Statistical Classification of Diseases and Related Health Problems, 10th Revision* (ICD-10) of the World Health Organization (2010). There are also substantial differences. For example, the ICD lists personality disorders in the same way as other disorders, whereas the DSM lists them on a separate axis. The ICD is ratified by all the WHO member countries. Compared with the DSM, which is primarily used in the United States, the ICD is used widely in Europe and other parts of the world. The ICD-11 is scheduled for publication in 2018.

According to the DSM, a syndrome describes a constellation of symptoms that either occur together or covary over time. A disorder refers to a cluster of symptoms. Like a syndrome, its causes are unclear. A disease refers to a disorder where the etiology (set of causes) is presumed to be known. The DSM-5 defines mental disorder as follows:

> A mental disorder is a syndrome characterized by clinically significant disturbance in an individual's cognition, emotion regulation, or behavior that reflects a dysfunction in the psychological, biological, or developmental processes underlying mental functioning. Mental disorders are usually associated with significant distress in social, occupational, or other important activities. An acceptable or culturally approved response to a common stressor or loss, such as the death of a loved one, is not a mental disorder. Socially deviant behavior (e.g., political, religious, or sexual) and conflicts between the individual and society are *not* mental disorders unless the deviance or conflict results from a dysfunction in the individual, as described above. (20; emphasis added)

We can see this definition indicates that mental disorder has multiple causes and that there are controversies over whether these causes are biological, psychological, social, cultural, or political, or whether a disorder has an etiology that is mental, or indicates a condition that impacts on mental functioning. Anthropologists have been at the forefront of criticisms about the ways culture is viewed as an explanation for mental illness, about the claims of the universality of biomedical categories, and about the ways psychiatry has become geared toward the efficacies of pharmaceutical treatments to the neglect of the social and political foundations of suffering. Additionally, they have been successfully engaged as writers of the DSM and have achieved changes to the codification of cross-cultural aspects of diagnosis and treatment in the DSM.

Approaches and Definitions

This book uses the term mental disorder over madness, which refers to severe psychotic states of mental illness; over insanity, which is a legal term; and over lunacy, which historically attributed madness to people's exposure to the moon. It takes as a given that these terms have shifting meanings. It also prioritizes the terms illness and disorder over disease. Thereby it builds on the legacy of the distinction that Arthur Kleinman (1988a: 3) made between illness as the "innately human experience of symptoms and suffering," related to the feeling or interpretation of being unwell, and "sickness" or disease, which refers to the underlying criteria or causes attributed to those feelings, usually in professional categories and usually contested. These languages of definitions, it holds, are central to ways conditions are understood and treated and to understanding societal attitudes toward mental disorder and its sufferers.

This book's title applies to psychiatric classifications, but importantly it also borrows conceptually from Byron Good's (2012a) category "disorder," which links individual, societal, and political forms of madness or disorder. Good (2012a) argues that the concept disorder is critical to the ethnography of subjectivity for medical and psychiatric anthropologists. In his article "Theorizing the 'Subject' of Medical and Psychiatric Anthropology," he makes four claims. First, anthropologists should attend to the national and global economic processes, violence, and modes of exclusion, "citizenship," **xv** and governance that produce "subtle modes of internalized anxieties that link subjection and subjectivity" (517). Thereby they can position the political at the heart of the psychological. This can mitigate the tendency of post-structuralist explanations to downplay the humanist subject in favor of analyses of the "subject position"—a tendency that results, Good argues, in "thick theory and thin ethnography" (517). Second, we can strengthen this political position by addressing the postcolonial and by analyzing the presence of colonialism in anthropology and in many societies where anthropologists work. This can link the madness of the state and individuals, collective and individual memories, repressions and remembering. It can also denote constructions of threats to order and force our attention to the often violent ways political, moral, and epistemic orders are established (518). Third, the term disorder can force our attention to the ways ideas, institutions, and modes of domination, such as God, science, capital, commerce, and so on, shape the modernist equation of disorder in opposition to a bourgeois colonial and postcolonial order (518). Fourth, we must attend to what is unsaid and borrow from psychoanalysis to ensure we do not "miss" what is hidden in plain view. This way we can locate the madness of the subject more completely in its everyday sites of eruption (523).

Another concern related to our topic is how to translate framings of mental disorder into diagnosis and treatment. Good (2012a: 523) proposes that "intervention" can be deployed as an ethical mode of inquiry for investigating psychotic illness and trauma. It can help build care systems around the inner lives of those treated. Translated into practice, the ideal of intervention can have positive consequences, especially in criticizing power relations in the ways the pathologies of underdeveloped, poor, postcolonial societies are used as a mandate for intervention by international organizations. This is important if our investigations are to have any effect on the people we research. Yet realities can be far from ideal, as we will see in many case studies in this book, especially in the structure and delivery of frontline psychiatry.

Good's approach is intellectually sophisticated, humane, and pragmatic. It infuses most chapters that follow, in spirit if not directly. The approach of this book builds on some important conceptual work by anthropologists. For example, Jerome Wakefield (2007) makes a distinction between biomedical and socio-political approaches. Wakefield identifies a basic division between value-laden and scientific approaches in "the degree of legitimacy in psychiatry's claims to be a truly medical discipline rather than, as anti-psychiatrists and others have claimed, a social control institution masquerading as a medical discipline" (150). He proposes the concept of "harmful dysfunction" to capture the *interaction* of a legitimate biological failure or organic dysfunction with a socio-cultural value judgment in the conceptualization of mental disorder (149). Emphatically, mental disorder is not a social construct. Florid psychosis, catatonic depression, and hearing voices are real, not constructs, and certainly not a choice. Rather than become mired in debates between "either-or" biological essentialism and social constructionism, it is important we emphasize the diverse attributions of meanings and causes that contribute to sufferers' experiences. Wakefield's argument about multiple interacting causes is an important premise of this book. It is important because it can be used to challenge the increasingly hegemonic view of mental illness as a "brain disease." The "brain disease-model" is the dominant approach in US psychiatry. So is the view that mental disorder is caused by a "disruption in neural circuits," as defined by the US National Institute of Mental Health (NIMH) (Insel 2011), the world's largest research organization on mental health. These dominant views imply that mental disorder is principally the result of a problem in brain functioning and based primarily on biological causes, downplaying social, cultural, or environmental factors.

Relatedly, many anthropologists have criticized the increasing dominance of bio-psychiatry as an explanation and a tool for treating societal problems. In their book *The Loss of Sorrow*, Horwitz and Wakefield (2007: 25) interrogate ways that modern psychiatry has been key in transforming the intensity of normal sadness—such as might follow a significant loss—into the symptoms of a depressive disorder, a dysfunctional pathology, and a dire public health problem demanding urgent policy responses. Their book is a seminal work in anthropology and psychiatry. It shares company in this regard with Kleinman's *Rethinking Psychiatry* (1988b) and Byron Good's *Medicine, Rationality and Experience* (1994). As a medic and an anthropologist, Arthur Kleinman is well positioned to provide important anthropological insights into psychiatric practice and research. Through his careful work on cross-cultural comparison, he challenges what he has described as the dehumanization and potential abuses arising from the "hubris in bureaucratically motivated attempts to medicalize the human condition" (1988: 17). In his work, Good (1994) argues that, far from superseding non-Western and folk medical systems, biomedicine's account of the human body and illness is a belief system akin to traditional healing systems.

Instead of accepting the dominance of biomedicine unquestioningly, we must analyze how physicians and healers come to inhabit culturally distinct worlds of moral meaning and experience, wherein illness narratives and bodily experience shape human suffering, objects of clinical intervention, and medical knowledge and practice (65).

The topic of mental disorder also involves some diverse intellectual and disciplinary approaches. Although not all of these are equally reflected in this book, they are important. Kohrt and Mendenhall (2015: 22–23) provide an excellent overview of these in their book *Global Mental Health: Anthropological Perspectives*. They summarize three key differences between psychological anthropology, medical anthropology, and cultural psychiatry. I will paraphrase these in some detail.

First, psychological anthropology emphasizes ideas of culture and personality by focusing on "normal," culturally appropriate patterns of thought and behavior. This approach links back to the structural anthropological analysis of cultural materials such as mythology, pioneered by Claude Lévi-Strauss, and the idea of human thought processes comprising binary oppositions such as rational/irrational, normal/abnormal, and so on.

Second, medical anthropology and cultural psychiatry approach ways social phenomena influence "abnormal" phenomena and analyze the role of social, political, economic, and health institutions in shaping definitions of normality and sickness. The related field of ethnopsychiatry, led by Devereux and Mars, studies local healing systems for mental illness and for cultural contributions to psychopathology. Devereux's (1980) definition of culture was rooted in psychoanalytic theory and ideas that universal unconscious conflicts are *socially* resolved. Devereux viewed shamans as neurotics and healing ceremonies as producing violent psychic conflicts. Rather than concur with Devereux's ideas about a "shamanistic complex," Lévi-Strauss emphasized the effects of the shaman's belief in his power to heal, the social group's and patient's belief in the shaman's power, and the likelihood the patient would be cured. Kohrt and Mendenhall then highlight the transcultural psychiatry movement, which began at McGill University in Canada in the 1950s. This movement regularly employs Western psychiatric categories to make cross-cultural comparisons and to analyze perspectives of symptom presentation, cultural influences on healing, and cultural consultation in clinical care.

Third, many critics view Western psychiatry itself as a cultural construct used to promote its own interests and the social control of a hegemonic state apparatus. These ideas are foundational to the "anti-psychiatry movement," whose roots originate in Foucault's historical analysis of "madness" and works by Szasz, Laing, and others. Politicized debates about the cross-cultural generalizability of disorders subsequently reformulated around the movement for global mental health (MGMH). For MGMH practitioners, tackling the increasing prevalence of mental health problems worldwide is an urgent agenda. They take biomedical psychiatric categories as the starting point for understanding and treating many disorders across the globe.

History and the Present

While much contemporary anthropological work on mental disorder has been built on these insights, some historicization is necessary. A good place to start is with Georges Canguilhem's classic book *The Normal and the Pathological* ([1966] 1991). Canguilhem argued that the emerging categories of modern biology and medicine were intertwined with political, economic, and technological imperatives. Canguilhem's work was an important influence on Michel Foucault. Foucault's book *Madness and Civilization* (1965) examined the emerging truths of psychopathology and their relation to power structures and community and to legal and religious institutions in late nineteenth-century France. In it, Foucault tells his readers a story about Parisian hospitals such as Hôpital Général and Salpêtrière. Since 1656, these institutions had confined the poor, homeless, criminal, and violently insane. Their inmates were punished and separated, and they were viewed as absolute in their difference from mainstream civilized society. Then, in the late eighteenth century, things began changing. French psychiatrists such as Pinel, Tuke, and later Charcot and the psychoanalyst Freud, introduced humanitarian reforms that brought medical advances to the treatment of the violently insane. These authorized new contacts between doctors and patients, who were now viewed as fully human. Thereby they treated patients' "alienation" and dispatched the deepest meanings of confinement. According to Foucault (1965: 504), "Mental illness, with all its familiar present connotations, then became possible." Similarly in the UK, the 1845 Lunacy Act transformed "lunatics"—and the criminally insane—into patients. Foucault emphasizes that "madness" is not a natural, fixed thing. Its meanings depend on the society in which it exists. These meanings are used to establish particular kinds of truth, and they translate into particular kinds of treatment, attitude, and reality for sufferers. The painting *Casa de locos* (*The Madhouse*) by the Spanish painter Francisco Goya (1819), which shows asylum patients as profoundly human and victims, has been interpreted as a denunciation of psychiatric institutions in Europe at that time.

We can find a good example of a Foucauldian-type analysis in Ian Hacking's book *Mad Travelers* (2002), in which he discusses the mental illness "fugue" that existed in nineteenth-century France. He demonstrates how cultural, medical, and societal understandings of madness all coalesce in the case of an obsessive traveler. Fugue describes a confluence of psychiatric dissociation, amnesia, and travel, which could only have emerged as a pathology because of the strict governmental checks and controls around movement at that time. Indeed, elsewhere Hacking (1999) argues against defining specific sciences at all, as they are in continual flux. He describes a "looping effect" whereby classifying people into types of normality or abnormality changes the fields of description, the possibilities of personhood, as well as the possibilities for sufferers of mental illness to transform dominant notions of the abnormal.

These types of analyses emphasize the social meanings and political governance of the ideas and categories of abnormality. Correspondingly, this book queries the extent to which normality and abnormality, and sanity and insanity, reside in patients or in the environments and contexts in which researchers and medics find them. It also asks how ideas of "culture" operate similarly. How, for example, can anthropology critique its own knowledge cultures in relation to contemporary ways of "dealing with culture"? One key challenge, as emphasized, is to capture *both* the reality of human suffering and the power relations that shape it. This involves seeing that there are other positions than either a radically constructionist or reductive biogenetic one. At the same time, falling into either position is not surprising given both "mental illness as a brain disorder" and the "myth of mental illness" are widely available cultural scripts.

In short, therefore, it is a key objective of this book to provide a critical overview of the shift from the explanations dominated by cultural and structural ecologies to those from biomedicine and clinical science, through time and across the globe. These shifts have enabled us to *link* the abstract approach of genetics and biomedicine on the one hand with social constructionism on the other. Anthropologists now work with the idea of "local biologies" (Lock 1993), and with the idea that social environments can leave "biomarkers" of specific local contexts. This is the idea behind research into socio-biology or, depending on the researcher's emphasis, biosociality. The current return to biology via new advances in brain studies, neuroscience, and epigenetics is not the whole story. Discussions are still normative. This means researchers are still debating what epigenetics actually is. While they agree it involves the way environmental factors cause genetic changes, the field needs more clarification. Are we talking about the study of gene–environment interactions or of heredity? The role of biology in mental disorders has met especially strong critiques from anthropologists, cultural psychiatrists, psychoanalysts, activists, and political movements. Some are fiercely "anti-biology" and see any biological explanation as too politicized, racialized, and essentializing. Others raise similarly strong objections to explanations of "culture." Even so, many practitioners look hopefully toward anthropologists in developing what they term "cultural competency." Cultural competency models emphasize effective engagement with people from other cultures. They are popular in health care, nursing, and with government agencies, but not without controversy. The medical anthropologist Jonathan Metzl (2012) strongly objects to training mental health professionals in cultural competency. He argues that emphasizing "culture" can obscure structural political-economic problems deriving from inequality, discrimination, and racism. Instead, he argues professionals should focus on "structural competency." This means situating the specificities of patient care within larger social inequalities of place, race, and economy. Paul Farmer (2005) similarly argues that anthropologists *must* keep analyses of structural violence up-front if they are to advance struggles for rights in public health and medicine and challenge ways professionalized responses to suffering become "pathologies of power."

Finally, this book questions the goals of therapy, treatment, and rehabilitation. What are our expectations of a "return to normality"? What kinds of wounds and healing are at play in ways that disordered realities are re-ordered? Does medicine's goal to "cure the symptom" mean we suppress rather than explore people's problems? This problem reminds us of ritual healing practices, which work *with* the symptom. The shaman or ritual healer is a classic figure who pushes us to question taken-for-granted assumptions about mental illness and recovery. This short book unfortunately gives short shrift to anthropology's immense contributions to understanding ritual healing, spirit worship and possession, religion and medicine, shamanism, and so on. However, it does raise one caution. When confronted with the schizophrenic as an exotic or romantic figure of religious, spiritual, or artistic authority, we should remember that the "madness" of severe delusional or psychotic states frequently involves such severe disturbance, disorganization, and unhappiness that many schizophrenics are simply too ill to serve as religious authorities.

Of course this short book cannot review the entire literature on mental disorder. Rather, its aim is to elaborate on some useful ways to interpret understandings of mental disorder involving anthropology. It does this by tracing some key debates through time, across social and cultural settings, through their geographical distribution across the globe, and through some illustrative case studies that subject some particular disorders to scrutiny. It queries ways social conditions, poverty, and oppressive relationships might interact to disproportionately expose certain populations to disease clusters. It also scrutinizes the mental health professions. In scrutinizing anthropology, it asks if we want to occupy a position of critique, collaboration, theoretical distance—or the more complicated position of "adjacency" (observing the observer observing while maintaining one's theoretical forms of inquiry) (Rabinow 2007). Will anthropologists "simply" observe, or will they use anthropological expertise and methods to consider the question, What would make life better for patients? If so, it will be important to stretch anthropology's traditional contribution. This has been to build knowledge slowly, over time, via individual researchers often working alone.

By the nature of their methods, anthropologists are also well positioned to query the idea of a critical window for intervention, the sense of urgency produced, and to reflect on the temporality in the politics of particular projects. By working collaboratively with other disciplines, we can go beyond the single snapshot, generate and answer questions about generalizability, and add specificity and depth to the rapid-assessment ethnographies that many professionals are asked to provide.

Anthropology's theoretical interests are constantly changing. Thus, one premise of this book is that mental disorder provides a "tool for thinking with" the transformation of anthropological knowledge, while connecting **xxi** it to traditional forms of scholarship, debate, and practical application. A summary outline of the book's chapters follows.

Book Outline

In order to prepare the ground for some debates that follow, Chapter 1 examines historical controversies surrounding the "culture concept" in anthropology. Anthropological work on "abnormality" allows us to explore some theoretical debates about cultural functionalism, cultural relativism, and the extent to which the culture concept is useful for mental disorder. Culture is more than a theoretical concept. It is also practically very important in regard to symptomology, to variations in ways mental distress is understood and treated, and in mapping shifting cultures of mental health practice such as the increasing medicalization of psychiatry. We can draw on our valuable historical knowledge cultures in order to more usefully approach all clinical work in terms of intercultural interaction, wherein different languages, religions, and healing systems interplay with structural and political factors.

Chapter 2 discusses some problems with the concept of culture in anthropology, which too often was used to describe inferior and exotic forms of difference involving non-Western, non-Euro-American Others. The role of culture as anthropology's radical Other became replaced by a focus on "the suffering subject" as the bridge between cultures. The chapter outlines some linkages of mental disorder to the pathological workings of global political and institutional power, and it highlights research on "social suffering" as one means anthropologists have sought to construct alternative languages of illness. It also shows how studies of the relationship between language and suffering have employed the single life story as a way to grasp the humanity of people affected by mental disorder.

Chapter 3 examines some connections of culture and psychiatry. It draws on examples from across the world to examine trends in the history of cultural psychiatry, including the origins of cultural psychiatry in colonialism, through contemporary forms of global and cultural psychiatry. Culture is referred to in its broadest sense to include cultures of psychiatry and the cultural assumptions that underpin the "psych" professions. The chapter additionally examines some formulations of culture and culture-bound syndromes within successive editions of the DSM, and some significant contributions that anthropologists have made to the formulation and treatment of culture in the DSM. Here, anthropologists have made key advances to thinking through what in psychiatric classifications is generally applicable and what is not, and thinking through problems of cultural and conceptual translation.

The next two chapters scrutinize some specific disorders. Chapter 4 examines some perspectives on trauma. Following the incorporation of post-traumatic stress disorder (PTSD) into the DSM-III in 1980, anthropological research largely focused on interpreting culturally specific variations and therapeutic responses. After the 1990s, more emphasis was placed on analyzing social and cultural mechanisms to understand how experiences were recognized as traumatic and how they were healed. Next came critiques leveled at the political uses and ascendancy of trauma in governing the structures and borders of the international legal system, military and humanitarian interventions, and policies around refugees, asylum seekers, and immigration control.

Chapter 5 addresses the "big three" most commonly diagnosed psychiatric disorders: schizophrenia, depression, and bipolar disorder. Schizophrenia and bipolar disorder have significant overlap in terms of psychosis. Both share symptoms of major clinical depression, and all three share a history of misunderstanding, clinical variations in cultural understandings, and assumptions of poor prognosis. The medical journalist Robert Whitaker (2003) argues that conditions for people with schizophrenia in the United States are far worse than in many of the world's poorest countries, and even worse than conditions for asylum patients in the nineteenth century. This chapter reviews some historical and modern classifications, and it reflects on a range of case studies of the "big three," including from Ireland, Japan, Bali, and modern America.

Chapter 6 elaborates perspectives on how global politics, Western psychiatric treatments, diagnostics, psychotic symptoms, and local community values interact. The powerful nexus between biopsychiatry and the pharmaceutical industry means there is pressure to "scale up" access to psychiatric treatments within the global South. At the same time, the dominance of psychiatry and pharmaceutical treatments is receiving increased criticism in the global North. The chapter also draws continuities between global mental health and colonialism and illustrates ways that disordered polities, political madnesses, and multiple violences have been theorized as "postcolonial disorders."

The focus of Chapter 7, which draws the book to a close, is on ideas of recovery, and particularly on ways therapeutic techniques shape new "orders" out of "disordered" realities. It begins by considering how markets for prescription drugs have expanded alongside ways people use legal and illegal drugs to manage mental distress throughout the life span, and how modern psychotropic drugs are shaping new forms of life. It also points to the shared history of psychiatry and religion, and to some current interrelations of pharmaceutical treatments and religious and spiritual modes of healing. It then continues the theme of subjectivity and language: as a mode of anthropological representation and as a therapeutic tool. For psychiatrists, the dominance of biomedical models and the decline of psychoanalytic psychiatry means that, for many, a minor intervention such as simply talking to people is no longer possible.

Discussion and Activities

Explain and distinguish the terms lunacy, madness, illness, sickness, disease, and disorder. What implications do the meanings of these terms hold for conceptualizing the subject of intervention?

In what particular ways might "traditional" and "Western" psychiatric-medical approaches to illness and healing coexist?

Even when illness classification and treatment systems seem radically different, can we find points of similarity? Do you think we can talk about "equivalences"?

How does the researcher's cultural positioning influence the interpretation of mental illness?

How does watching an ethnographic film differ from reading a text in ways we might understand mental disorder?

Additional Film and Readings

Film

Shadows and Illuminations. 2010. Directed by Robert Lemelson. *Afflictions: Culture and Mental Illness in Indonesia*. Anthropology and Psychiatry Film Series. Watertown, MA: Documentary Educational Resources.

Readings

Canguilhem, Georges. 2012. *Writings on Medicine*. New York: Fordham University Press.

Desjarlais, Robert. 1994. "Struggling Along: The Possibilities for Experience among the Homeless Mentally Ill." *American Anthropologist* 96: 886–901.

Foucault, Michel. 1975. *I, Pierre Rivière, Having Slaughtered my Mother, my Sister, and my Brother...: A Case of Parricide in the 19th Century*. Lincoln: University of Nebraska Press.

Foucault, Michel. 1965. *Madness and Civilization: A History of Insanity in the Age of Reason.* Translated by Richard Howard. London: Tavistock.

Lemelson, Robert B. 2004. "Traditional Healing and Its Discontents: Efficacy and Traditional Therapies in Neuropsychiatric Disorders in Bali." *Medical Anthropology Quarterly* 18: 48–76.

Lock, Margaret, and Vihn-Kim Nguyen, eds. 2007. *An Anthropology of Biomedicine.* Oxford: Wiley-Blackwell.

Mendenhall, Emily. 2012. *Syndemic Suffering: Social Distress, Depression and Diabetes among Mexican Immigrant Women.* Walnut Creek, CA: Left Coast Press.

Scull, Andrew. 2015. *Madness in Civilisation: A Cultural History of Insanity, from the Bible to Freud, from the Madhouse to Modern Medicine.* Princeton, NJ: Princeton University Press.

Suryani, L.K., and Jensen, G. 1995. *Trance and Possession in Bali: A Window on Western Multiple Personality Disorder, Possession Disorder, and Suicide.* New York: Oxford University Press.

Whitaker, Robert. 2003. *Mad in America. Bad Science, Bad Medicine, and the Enduring Mistreatment of the Mentally Ill.* New York: Perseus Publications.

CHAPTER 1

CULTURE, ABNORMALITY, AND DISORDER

This largely theoretical chapter introduces perspectives that place "culture" at the heart of mental disorder. It queries some historical knowledge cultures and approaches to culture, as well as formations of "biology" and "structure" in anthropology. It asks what anthropology can reveal about ways "culture" creates subjects and understandings of abnormality. The example of schizophrenia reveals how debates around the relative importance of culture, biology, and environment play out in contemporary cultures of mental health practice, treatment, and recovery. Last is the cultural shift in psychiatry, from its foundations in psychoanalysis to a system dominated by biomedical explanations and treatments.

Let us turn first to Ruth Benedict, a student of Franz Boas, the "Father of American Anthropology." In her article entitled "Anthropology and the Abnormal" (1934a), Benedict queries the extent to which abnormality describes people's inability to function socially or if it is a function of culture. She distinguishes between "sick individuals" and "sick civilizations," and she argues that abnormality is "caused" by the individual's inability to bear the particular pressures of culture placed upon him or her (60). Benedict sees normality as being in various ways culturally defined, created, and valued. What is "abnormal" from a Eurocentric point of view may be quite "normal" and valued in another culture. Drawing on reflections from American Indian tribes, Siberian shamans, South African Zulus, and from Dubu Island in Melanesia, she makes the following statement: "It is clear that culture may value and make socially available even highly unstable human types. If it chooses to treat their peculiarities as the most valued variants of human behavior, the individuals in question will rise to the occasion" (64). Benedict means if mental instability is somehow made to usefully serve the functioning of a particular culture, it is not a problem. It may even become valued. She continues, "The culture, according to its major preoccupations, will increase and intensify hysterical, epileptic, or paranoid symptoms, at the same time relying socially in a greater and greater degree upon these very individuals (75).

Benedict (1934a) also made similar arguments about Western cultures, "here" where "we" live. She describes how "unbridled and arrogant egoists as family men, as officers of the law, and in business ... are extreme types of personality configurations, ... which according to any absolute category would be regarded abnormal" (75–76). She draws comparisons with other cultures where many "abberants" also perform roles of authority and leadership. Benedict pays attention to the figure of the shaman, in whom she sees abnormal behaviors honored and attributed with curative spiritual power becoming "the outstanding characteristic of the most respected social type, the type which functioned with most honor and reward in the community" (62).

For Benedict (1934a), the actual type of abnormality is not important. Instead it is the individual's exclusion from participation in recognized patterns of society that makes abnormality a problem. If the individual can resolve the pressures of the cultural expectations he or she faces, it is possible to function adequately (75). One point is that Benedict did acknowledge her argument applied best to the high-functioning "unstable human type" rather than individuals who are not able to function well socially. Her arguments are typical of the cultural functionalist tradition. There are many criticisms of this approach; for example, that it ignores those inequalities around gender, class, race, and so on that produce inner societal tensions and lead to social change rather than reproduce fixed forms of cultural functioning.

In 1934 Benedict also published her book *Patterns of Culture* ([1934b] 2005). This advanced her view of human culture as being like an individual "personality writ large": "A culture, like an individual, is a more or less consistent pattern of thought and action" (46). Benedict saw each culture as having a "personality" that is encouraged in each individual. Particular characteristics are selected from the vast array of human potentialities. They become the leading personality traits of the people living in that culture, and they contribute to an interdependent complex societal whole. Thus, a culture may be paranoid, megalomaniac, or pathological in some other way. This view typifies the "culture and personality school," among whom Edward Sapir and Margaret Mead were also prominent. Along with Benedict, these figures were criticized for equating individual personalities with collective processes and for neglecting to analyze interactions of individual characteristics and changing historical conditions.

In his book *Medicine, Rationality and Experience*, Byron Good (1994: 31–36) also reflects on some anthropological work on normality and abnormality. He offers some thoughts on Benedict's legacy. He points out that Benedict's argument still continues to challenge theories about the relation of cultural representation and disease, particularly her view that the "borderline" between normal and abnormal is culturally formulated, that social responses have the power to amplify pathology, and that abnormality and pathology are inseparable from cultural interpretation (35). Of less endurance is her understanding that psychopathology is essentially a problem of adjustment, and that the shamans of many societies would be considered disordered or even schizophrenic, which has been largely abandoned (34). Nonetheless, Benedict's proposition that some societies develop highly elaborate forms of psychopathology has been expanded under the broad rubric of "culture-bound disorders," although her hypotheses about the extent of cultural variation, particularly in relation to schizophrenia and manic depression, have not withstood investigation. There is also the unfortunate consequence of her use of labels such as "paranoid" or "megalomaniac." Benedict used these to describe whole cultures. Although she may have intended to indicate that our own labels for pathology are culture-bound and relative, she ended up pathologizing wholesale the cultures that she wrote about (35).

What Is "Culture"?

Let us historicize some of these issues about culture in anthropology. The concept raises interesting questions. Do we make culture, does culture make us, or both? Does everybody have culture, or just peoples belonging to "other cultures"? What do anthropologists try to do when they describe, interpret, and represent culture? What kinds of power relations do representations of culture entail?

Historically, anthropological representations of "culture," and their relation to the equally unwieldy terms "biology" and "structure," have been characterized by oppositions. Dichotomies between "their beliefs" and "our knowledge," primitivism and rational science, and so on were constructed around culture as a monolithic, static system. Criticisms of these oppositions were partly inspired by earlier critiques of anthropology's role in colonialism. British structural-functional anthropology, for example, was at the forefront in developing ideas about traditional "primitive" cultures. Rivers, Radcliffe-Brown, and Evans-Pritchard all reified traditional cultures as if they occurred in pure form and had existed in isolation for centuries as static, immobile structures. Cultural relativists such as Boas and Benedict recognized the damage inherent in such representations. They argued that non-Western cultures should be seen as equal but different. However, they still exaggerated the differences between societies. Morever, the differences they identified were not always as "equal" as others might have wished.

The deployment of culture to pathologize so-called inferior (usually non-white, colonized or immigrant) groups has an insidious legacy in the work of human scientists such as Sir Francis Galton, the English Victorian anthropologist, pioneer eugenicist, geneticist, and tropical explorer. Galton (1869) studied the inheritance of intelligence between races ("naturally" the white races were more intelligent), and he coined the term "nature versus nurture." Galton supported racial segregation, anti-miscegenation laws, forced sterilization, and the eugenic science of improving inefficient human stock with better strains. Explanations involving culture, biology, and environment are clearly political. It is important not to separate these phenomena. For example, severe forms of mental illness may be inherited and biological, but we also inherit our parents' environments and their cultural, national, and personal histories.

In the 1960s and 1970s there was a turn away from biological determinism toward cultural phenomenology, which now constructed the Other as shaped by diverse cultural and behavioral environments. Two "manifestos" from the early 1970s shifted anthropologists' attention from "function" toward "meaning." First, Clifford Geertz (1977) asserted anthropologists should examine culture as a product of active social beings trying to find meaning in the world. For Geertz, anthropologists *interpret* culture. More radically, Roy Wagner (1975) asserted that anthropologists *invent* culture in their writing and attempts to make sense of different societies. Both Geertz and Wagner wrote about culture in the context of societies that anthropologists represented as being radically "alien" to their own. This question about "invention" led to claims that anthropologists objectified cultures as bounded wholes in their records of non-Western peoples, and paid insufficient attention to ways ideas and meanings are rooted in relations of power. The position was famously developed in Edward Said's (1978) book *Orientalism*. Said emphasized predominant Western ideas of the "Orient," its irrationality, fundamentalism, exoticism, unruliness, and female oppression. He drew parallels with representations of other places as "primitive," "tribal" "savage," and "exotic." This in turn led to "writing (against) culture" work in the 1980s and 1990s (see, for example, Abu-Lughod 1991; Bakhtin 1986; Clifford and Marcus 1986; Ong 1987; Poewe 1996; Spencer 1989; Street and Thompson 1993). This anthropological work inspired experimentation to address perceived limitations in "traditional" ethnographies and to pursue new agendas of representation.

More recently, Bruce Kapferer (2013) revisited the origins of "exoticism" in defining human populations considered marginal to imperialism and colonial authority. He proposes that, despite its obvious controversies, the concept has critical and innovative potential (814–15). Kapferer argues that Darwin's discovery of evolution crucially opened up the notion of the *scientific exotic*, which began the tradition of using the exotic as a radical way to challenge dominant modes of thought (818). Subsequently, the exotic developed as a way to give serious expression to marginalized, suppressed, or subordinated practices, in other words the "minor discourse." The "minor discourse" was prominently epitomized in Lévi-Strauss's "Tristes Tropiques" ([1955] 1992). The criticism of the "minor discourse," however, is that it reproduces the very dualisms—for example, major/minor, East/West, madness/sanity, and so on—that it protests (Kapferer 2013, 823). Despite these problems, Kapferer (2013) argues that we can and should develop the exotic conceptually and methodologically to reveal dynamics that are suppressed by ruling understandings (833).

Concerning the relation of culture and biology, the emphasis on "nature" and its relation to "culture" is an ongoing concern for anthropologists. Some approaches emphasize a nature-culture dichotomy, where nature shapes culture or vice versa. Others challenge the nature-culture distinction altogether. Philippe Descola (2013), who was a student of Lévi-Strauss, argues that the culture-nature dualism tends to construct humans as superior and external to nature. He views the very idea that nature provides a sort of backdrop to "culture" or a stage on which humans act as characteristic of anthropology's "imperialist arrogance" and "incipient racism" (66). Instead he proposes we should analyze culture and nature as part of a single whole. This approach makes sense in the light of subsequent developments in our discipline.

It bears on the question of how anthropology can critique its own knowledge cultures in relation to advances in the natural sciences. Certainly, many anthropologists are questioning what concepts we might borrow from biological sciences to understand the role of culture in mental disorder. Biological anthropologists have developed many interesting methods to investigate the socio-cultural and biological formation of mental disorders (Dressler 2012; Kohrt et al. 2013; Worthman and Panter-Brick 2008). "Bioethnographic" methods have also been proposed to explore the biosociality of intergenerational trauma ("soft heredity"), and ways centuries of classed and racialized privilege *do* change biology ("hard heredity"). These concerns, we have stressed, are all highly political. For example, why do studies of "bio-sociality" overwhelming biosocialize the poor? The questions have a long tradition. They concerned Franz Boas, for example, who was passionate about fighting racial inequality, which he viewed as social, not biological, in origin.

While this book does not engage in great detail with knowledge produced by genetics or neuroscience, anthropologists and other social scientists are actively engaged in work that is, in one way or another, biosocial. This would include the biocultural approaches that Daniel Lende and Greg

Downey (2012) developed under the rubric of "neuroanthropology," the "critical neuroscience" advocated by Jan Slaby and Suparna Choudhury (2011), and the "ecology of mind" outlined by Laurence Kirmayer (2015). Kirmayer (2015) offers a comprehensive summary of ways to think through interactions of the place of phenomenology in psychiatric practice and research, advances in cognitive and social neuroscience, the development of social-ecological and cultural models of mental disorders, and the challenges of responding to global mental health disparities (624)—and notably, a "cultural neurophenomenology" that can examine how cultural knowledge interacts with neurobiological and psychological responses in experiences of affliction, healing, resilience, and recovery (627).

One interesting example of bioethnographic research comes from the First Thousand Days Research Group (Pentecost 2016). This project builds on knowledge in neuroscience, epigenetics, and developmental origins of health and disease research. Its premise is that the first thousand days between conception and a child's second birthday are critical to its future health and potential. In a range of settings across southern Africa, the group combines ethnographic research in antenatal clinics, soup kitchens, laboratories of reproductive technologies, places of worship, neonatal units, breast milk banks, middle-class settings, and informal settlements, using indices such as the offspring's birth weight, nutritional data, and cognitive development. Thereby it seeks new understandings of the neuroscience of cognition and the developmental origins of health and disease—now commonly framed as epigenetic—and their impact on economic outcomes, reproductive technologies, nutrition interventions, the law, understandings of time and inheritance, the making of families, the meaning of food security, and understandings of health and life.

These developments all address the important task of how to disentangle "culture" from environmental, structural, and population factors. Many practitioners ask anthropologists to develop ways of dealing with cultural issues in communities. It is of practical importance, therefore, that we find ways to influence policy and advocacy. Culture engages shifting meanings in many different fields of practice. In science it poses interesting questions for cultural psychiatrists about the brain and mental functioning. It certainly bears on ways that environments affect mental illness, people's access to health care, and on the ethical dilemmas facing clinicians who must decide which treatments are optimal for particular communities. Denying people opportunities to practice their culture also raises human rights issues. Culture is intrinsically political when "multicultural" policies reproduce hierarchies and intolerance and inferiorize minority, immigrant, or marginalized groups. "Culture," in short, is a real mental health stressor, and it links politically to addressing the needs of vulnerable people.

Reflections on Schizophrenia

More concretely, let us explore some cultures of knowledge and representation in relation to schizophrenia, deemed the most severe of mental disorders. Schizophrenia is also expanded on in Chapter 5.

Schizophrenia has been diversely attributed to biological, cultural, environmental, and religious causes. Benedict (1934a) argues that among the Indian tribes of California, cataleptic seizures associated with schizophrenia were a means by which affectees could assume great power and importance as shamanic healers. She writes, "Cultural approval had seized upon them and made of them those who functioned with the most honor and reward in the community. It was precisely the cataleptic individuals who in this culture were singled out for authority and leadership" (62). For Benedict, schizophrenia is not a matter of biological inherited tendency, but quite simply an affair of social patterning and cultural functioning (79).

After the 1960s, functionalist explanations gave way to arguments about dysfunction. Particularly, they emphasized dysfunctional family systems. Gregory Bateson (1972) analyzed family communication structures and proposed a "double-bind" theory of impossible family relationships in which chronic cross-purposes and deliberate misunderstanding *caused* schizophrenia (205). This view that families caused schizophrenia was also the subject of the book by Theodore Lidz, Stephen Fletcher, and Alice Cornelison, *Schizophrenia and the Family* (1965), which propagated the concept of the dominant, rejecting, schizophrenogenic (or "refrigerator") mother. Although Lidz and colleagues argued parents caused schizophrenia, they sympathized with the stigma they suffered (in their own terms, a rather schizophrenogenic characteristic). Their ideas echoed those of anti-psychiatrists such as R.D. Laing (1964) who saw kindness and love in family relations as strategies to exert power and control (e.g., I love you, but it will be impossible for you to earn that love). Living in the era of Cold War hostility, Laing linked schizophrenia to societal struggles for power and control. He saw schizophrenia as a sane response to an insane world. For Laing, schizophrenia was a theory, or label, not a fact. Over time, Laing's own behavior became increasingly disorganized, leading people to deem him a madman, prophet, and mystic himself. Laing blamed parents and also society for schizophrenia, and he ignored any organic basis. These explanations met strong resistance from activist groups such as the Parents of Adult Schizophrenics. Formed in the United States in 1974, this group was successful in advocating and achieving changes to the ways schizophrenia was understood and treated.

By contrast, Jonathan Metzl analyzes schizophrenia as a social, political, or "structural" disorder in *The Protest Psychosis* (2010). Structure here refers to modes of racialized inequality, discrimination, and exclusion. Metzl traces the emergence of schizophrenia in the United States through the early twentieth century as a predominantly white middle-class women's problem to its transformation after the 1960s as one of "black insanity." Offering compelling examples from advertisements for antipsychotic medications that depict angry black men and African tribal symbols, which in turn played to civil rights–era anxieties about racial protest, his argument is that the overdiagnosis of "black" schizophrenia reflects a history of white institutional racism (202). That is, more black people were diagnosed with schizophrenia because of racism. Metzl was subjected to strong criticism by the anthropologist Tanya Luhrmann (2010) for glossing over ways that lived experiences of racism, stress, and trauma *do* produce higher rates of mental illness: "Why is it that racial prejudice, which certainly exists, seems so much more palatable as an explanation for high rates of illness than the effects of social inequality?" she asks (478). By attributing to or blaming on racism the increased rates of schizophrenia among the poor, minorities, and migrants, and among those suffering disability or financial debt, Luhrmann argues we simplify the picture and lose sight of the need to research ways schizophrenia is shaped socially, genetically, and epigenetically—and, we should add, politically.

Subsequently, the rise of genetic research recast schizophrenia as a biological disease. This absolved parents of responsibility for causing their children's schizophrenia. Nonetheless, many controversies still prevail around biological explanations. The clinical psychiatrist Robert Freedman (2009: 114–15) argues schizophrenia is produced by a neuronal inability to filter out incoming sensory experiences. He sees schizophrenia as a problem of brain function becoming increasingly beyond control, one of neuronal "excess." To prevent recurrent episodes of psychosis, more sophisticated pharmacological treatments are required to act on the dopaminergic system and individuals' stress response systems. For Freedman the solution is in better drugs.

There have been many contradictory definitions of schizophrenia, over 40 in all, leading Mary Boyle (2002) to describe schizophrenia as a "scientific delusion." Making some interesting connections between genetic science and spirit possession, Boyle (2004) also develops the idea of "genetic possession." She carefully interrogates "the idea there is a genetic disorder called schizophrenia" and scrutinizes the available research evidence, which she proposes is based on "selectively reported results, often from inappropriate statistics, as well as a failure to apply appropriate analysis" (81). She argues that the lack of evidence for genetic markers gave way to an emphasis on twin and adoption studies whose statistical and evidential failures could be more elaborately concealed (83). The lack of critical thinking around many genetic explanations, and the frequent making of assertions about genetics and schizophrenia, which bear no relationship to actual data, all conspired to strengthen the uncritical acceptance of schizophrenia as a genetic brain disorder. This supports psychiatry's claims to belong to the medical profession as well as funding for genetic and brain-based research. To elaborate, in the 1970s, scientists insisted schizophrenia was a physical disease. This approach allowed them to distance themselves from unfashionable "irrational" ideas involving mystical possession by ancestors, demons, deities, or animal spirits (79). However, these ideas have returned now in a new cultural form, that of "genetic possession." This involves the idea of something beyond our control and alien to our personal identity or responsible self. In much the same way people thought about the mysticism of spirit possession beliefs, for Boyle, genetic explanations seem to deprive intelligent people of all their critical faculties and to lay the cultural ground for "the uncritical acceptance of genetic research in schizophrenia regardless of its quality" (85).

Let us return a moment to the question of how economic conditions influence schizophrenia, particularly recovery. Some important studies dating back to the mid-twentieth century compared outcomes for recovery from schizophrenia in developing and developed nations (see especially reviews by Hopper 2004; 2007; Hopper et al., 2007; Jenkins and Barratt 2004; Luhrmann 2007). These are also important regarding anthropologists' engagements outside the discipline in relation to schizophrenia, in this case with psychiatric epidemiology. A controversial series of WHO studies conducted between the 1960s and 1990s showed "better outcomes" for people suffering from schizophrenia in "developing" versus "developed" countries. In other words, "No matter whether you look at symptoms, disability, clinical profile, or the ability to do productive work, people diagnosed with schizophrenia are far more likely to meet criteria for recovery in the developing world than in the developed world" (Luhrmann 2007: 145). The most robust of these data came from India, including the city Chennai, which is far from a romantic and rural idyll alien to Western contexts but a teeming, chaotic urban center. Here, both at 10- and 20-year follow-ups, two-thirds of patients remained largely symptom and medication free (Luhrmann 2007: 145).

These unexpected results are still not well understood and have sparked much interest among anthropologists. Luhrmann (2007: 144–47) offers two explanations that are frequently given. First, it is possible that patients in the developing countries did not all have schizophrenia but rather forms of remitting psychosis that suddenly onset and then got better. Second, there may be explanations related to "culture"; for example, involving family support and assistance during treatment; extended family households that allow some members to contribute without earning; low expressed emotion within families possibly related to more hallucinations in the apparently normal population; different levels of stigma attached to mental illness;

fewer pressures associated with entry-level jobs; and greater possible affinities of hallucinations with religious practice. However, these avenues, and the influence of culture, remain underresearched, nonspecified, and undisaggregated. Luhrmann's third explanation is that normative treatments of schizophrenia in our culture may actually make things worse by creating the conditions for chronicity and social defeat. Jablensky and Sartorius (2008) (who were involved in the WHO studies) raise other issues: the original outcomes were not uniformly better; opposite trends were also identified; the diagnostic criteria used were dated and nonstandardized; and the cited erosion of social support systems associated with globalization in high-income countries was underelaborated.

The WHO studies were also an important prelude to subsequent debates surrounding global mental health (Chapter 6). They urge much-needed caution around reducing mental illness outcomes to single variables related to development indicators, uncritical narratives about the developing world's urgent need for Western-type recovery systems, and assumptions that people always do better in the West.

"Of Two Minds?"

In this book, I devote considerable space to examining some epistemic cultures, and assumptions and pressures shaping contemporary psychiatry. Intellectual debates about culture certainly influence psychiatrists' views of patients, their diagnoses, and treatment decisions. Contemporary systems of mental health practice likewise have their own particular cultures and history. Next, I examine the important shift in psychiatry from its foundations in psychoanalysis to a system now dominated by the "culture" of biomedical explanations and treatments.

The twentieth century saw a profound shift away from the influence of psychoanalysis and from understandings of the underlying symptoms, logic, and structures of madness that were emphasized in early twentieth-century psychiatry. In classical psychiatry, distinctions between normality and madness were less pronounced than they are today. Take the example of psychosis. British psychoanalyst Darian Leader (2011: 11) emphasizes that many people have "ordinary psychosis" (also known as "white," "lucid," "everyday," "normal," and "private" psychosis) and live perfectly normal lives. That is, they may be "mad" without going mad. Freud ([1894] 1966) also viewed psychosis and delusions as not necessarily constituting madness. He thought they describe people's positive attempts to communicate distress and recover their natural state. Laing (1964) later attributed psychosis with cathartic and transformative potential. Despite these historical arguments, psychiatry moved toward much stronger distinctions between normal and abnormal states. Based on observable behavioral criteria, these largely moved away from earlier, psychoanalytically informed work of twentieth-century psychiatry.

In a fascinating study of this shift, Tanya Luhrmann's book *Of Two Minds* (2001) explores the "classic split" between biomedical and psychoanalytic approaches, or between pharmaceutical and talking cures, in American psychiatry. Luhrmann pays particular attention to the bifurcation of Axis 1 and Axis 2 type disorders in the DSM. Axis 1 includes schizophrenia, major depression, bipolar disorder, PTSD, and dissociative and obsessive-compulsive disorders. These "clinical syndromes" are putatively lifelong, "biological" in origin, and more severe (46). On the other hand, Axis 2 refers to neurotic disorders originating in psychoanalytic traditions, including personality and mood disorders such as borderline, narcissistic, bipolar (without psychosis), schizoid, and anti-social behaviors (47). These are seen as less severe and even as morally dubious. Psychiatrists-in-training learn to diagnose disorders in the DSM by matching given symptoms on a "diagnostic checklist." Many trainees are deeply skeptical about this method at the outset, but they eventually learn to "intuit" disorders with snapshot precision (35). This method serves to impose false distinctions between classificatory types, to downplay differences between patients' accounts and abstract itemized diagnoses, and to privilege the methodology of physiologic medicine, even though psychiatrists (at the time Luhrmann was writing) took no physiologic measurements (35). The regrettable consequences is that although "for most patients and most disorders, psychopharmacology and psychotherapy work best in combination … a combination of socio-economic forces and ideology is driving psychotherapy out of psychiatry" (23).

Drawing on ethnography with psychiatrists, psychiatrists-in-training, psychiatric nurses, and patients in the 1990s, Luhrmann (2001) documents how the "brutal experience" of training leads young doctors to gradually view the patients they see with hostility and detachment (84). Patients diagnosed with Axis 2 disorders become seen as manipulative, deceitful, and morally culpable compared with those with "real," morally respectable Axis 1 disorders, which are treatable with medication (115). The paradox in the biomedical model is that the more knowledge that doctors acquire, the less convinced they become that mental illness is a simple disease process (54). In turn, psychoanalytic trainees initially feel hollowed out, drained, angry, and emotionally disturbed by their patients—until they finally learn to "really see" how the theory works in action (153). Luhrmann shows, through rich ethnographic examples and vignettes, how the method of training reinforces the division between approaches, leading many psychiatrists to infer that psychoanalysis has failed (262). Toward the end of her book, Luhrmann discusses how American psychiatry became further transformed by the impacts of the "crisis of managed care," meaning that patients must increasingly negotiate the terms of care they receive with private health insurance companies. This is a startling insight into the way America's financial institutions are shaping the future of psychiatry and its delivery. That is, "the more time they [doctors] spend on the phone with insurance agents negotiating for a six-day admission to be extended to nine days because a patient is still suicidal, the more admissions interviews they need to do, the more discharge summaries they need to type, the less the ways of thought and experience of psychodynamic psychiatry fit in" (238). She summarizes,

12   The story of twentieth-century psychiatry is that psychoanalysis was important in Europe at a time when the approach to mental illness was essentially custodial. Psychoanalysis rapidly became entrenched as *the* theory that explained mental illness and *the* treatment that would cure it. Like most single answer cures, it overpromised. When new pharmacological treatments and theories emerged and successfully treated what psychoanalysis could not, the new psychiatric science came to win the ideological battle and to supplant its former rival. To the new adherents, psychoanalysis was charlatanry and psychiatric disorder was brain dysfunction. The psychoanalysts responded in kind. In practice, the more biomedical and the more psychodynamic approaches settled down in the 1980s into what one senior clinician called a "happy pluralism." Then the economic currents changed. As managed care companies began to take control over insurance reimbursements, the ideological tension between the psychopharmacological and psychoanalytic looked as if it presented a choice, and psychopharmacological approaches seemed cheaper and more like the rest of medicine. Compared to the power of these economic forces, the ideological tensions seem like domestic squabbles. But together they are pushing the psychodynamic approach out of psychiatry with a nearly irresistible force. (Luhrmann 2001: 203)

Luhrmann's prognosis, drawn from the 1990s, was arguably pessimistic. The heavy emphasis on biomedical models may also leave readers with the impression that talk therapy no longer exists when, in fact, psychiatrists work with psychologists and other "talk therapists" quite regularly. Chapter 7 discusses some of these. While biomedical models certainly dominate US, European, and global psychiatry, psychotherapies have also expanded. While psychoanalysis is long, expensive, and largely the preserve of clients who can afford it, humanistic, integrative, person-centered, family sys-temic, and cognitive behavioral therapies and counseling are all commonly used in public and private practice, and effectively tackle a variety of ills. "Nontraditional" techniques such as mindfulness, Buddhist, and Eastern therapies, as well as ecotherapy and other nature therapies are also popular.

To conclude, the history of culture in anthropology highlights its importance to understandings of mental disorder. Culture is not a given artifact or variable causing or driving mental illness. Anthropologists are not in the business of causality. Rather, our key questions concern how to productively link experiences of mental illness and mental health care provision to the multiple layers of context in which they are embedded. This means we do take seriously the psychotic's subjectivity, the reality status of delusion, and the mechanisms that link the individual to formations of the collective. We also query why mental illness rates, including those for schizophrenia, are higher in deprived and marginalized populations, not to repeat essentialized notions of deficient "culture" or biological "race" but to highlight how cultural explanations are used to obscure the embeddedness of a mentally ill person within the context of discrimination and structural violence.

13

Discussion and Activities

What characteristics mark the differences between so-called primitive, tribal, and modern societies? How do "nature" and the human body and mind feature within different portraits of "primitive culture"?

Can the concept of culture be sufficiently distinguished from racist discourses in anthropology? Discuss.

Bring examples of representations of anthropology, tribal groups, primitivism, or exoticism in popular culture (e.g., objects, masks, photographs, newspaper clips, magazines, advertisements, fashion or musical products, films, consumer packaging). Use these examples to discuss the role of culture, cultural texts, and industries, sciences, and the academy in the construction of the Other. Apply your discussion to framings of mental disorder.

Research and complete the 20 items on Canadian psychologist Robert Hare's "Psychopathy Checklist" (PCL-R). Assess the claim that "psychopathic" tendencies are disproportionately found among CEOs, political leaders, and big business entrepreneurs—that success in these worlds requires high scores of superficial charm; grandiosity; manipulative behavior; pathological lying; lack of remorse, empathy, or responsibility for one's actions; impulsivity; and promiscuous sexual behavior.

Is the concept of "culture" useful or a hindrance to understandings of mental disorder?

Additional Film and Readings

Film

Bird Dancer. 2010. Directed by Robert Lemelson. Afflictions: Culture and Mental Illness in Indonesia. Anthropology and Psychiatry Film Series. Watertown, MA: Documentary Educational Resources.

Readings

Bhabha, Homi K. 1994. *The Location of Culture*. New York: Routledge.

Horwitz, Allan, and Jerome Wakefield. 2007. *The Loss of Sorrow*. New York: Oxford University Press.

Jenkins, Janis. 2015. *Extraordinary Conditions. Culture and Experience in Mental Illness*. Berkeley: University of California Press.

Kirmayer, Laurence J., Robert Lemelson, and Constance Cummings, eds. 2015. *Re-Visioning Psychiatry: Cultural Phenomenology, Critical Neuroscience, and Global Mental Health*. Cambridge: Cambridge University Press.

Kohrt, Brandon, and Emily Mendenhall. 2015. "Historical Background: Medical Anthropology and Global Mental Health." In *Global Mental Health: Anthropological Perspectives*, edited by Brandon Kohrt and Emily Mendenhall, 19–36. Walnut Creek, CA: Left Coast Press.

Laing, R.D. 1964. *Sanity, Madness and the Family*. London: Penguin.

Szasz, Thomas. 1979. *Schizophrenia: The Sacred Symbol of Psychiatry*. Oxford: Oxford University Press.

Taussig, Michael. 1987. *Shamanism, Colonialism and the Wild Man: A Study in Terror and Healing*. Chicago: University of Chicago Press.

14

CHAPTER 2

BEYOND CULTURE TO THE SUFFERING SUBJECT

This chapter traces ways that problems associated with the culture concept led anthropologists to focus on the "suffering subject" and on individual experience as a way to grasp the "humanity" of people affected by mental disorder. Work by medical and social anthropologists that focuses on the concept of "social suffering" also highlights ways structural and political violence become collectively embodied in mental illness. This raises questions about power and language, the potential in different orders of explanation for "misreading" ways people inhabit worlds of suffering, and the possibilities afforded by social science critique for useful action.

By way of introducing and also framing this chapter, Joel Robbins's article "Beyond the Suffering Subject" (2013) describes how the demise of anthropology that studied the Other in cultural terms was widely acknowledged by the end of the 1980s. After the early 1990s, the subject living in pain, poverty, or violence and oppression emerged as "a new figure of humanity united in its shared vulnerability to suffering" (448). This figure enabled us to eschew "an anthropological world that had no place for savages," and to make sense of people who were living out the trauma of colonization and cultural loss (453). Robbins addresses anthropology's historical study of the primitive, savage, and exotic Other, and its struggles to move beyond this critique without losing the cultural specificity characterizing its theories and methods. He proposes "suffering slot anthropology" as one broadly based on empathic connection, moral witnessing, and human unity. While this approach can overcome problems associated with the culture concept, the focus on "universal suffering" may mean we lose some strengths of earlier work on the cultural aspects of the Other (453). Instead, we need to take the promise "suffering slot anthropology" implicitly offers: there must be better lives than the experiences of hopeless inadequacy and suffering it documents. Robbins argues that an "anthropology of the good" can deploy studies of value, morality, well-being, empathy, care, hope, change, and so on, not naively but positively, to seriously contest structures of violence, deprivation, and suffering. Rather than jettison the culture concept, it can and should usefully provide specificity to people's ideas of well-being and ideals.

16   Representing key studies that can link the anthropology of suffering with some grand transformations in ways the West understands itself, Robbins cites Didier Fassin and Richard Rechtman (2009) who propose that the human suffering from trauma has come to embody a "universal humanity," heeding neither cultural nor geographical borders. Next, he cites E. Valentine Daniel (1996) who draws on the stories of two brothers in the Sri Lankan civil war to argue that the suffering one endures as a victim or witness to violence is "culturally unrecuperable"—it does not require cultural interpretation to render experience sensible, but reminds us of the need as *human beings* to resist violence (372). Linking suffering and pleasure is the work by Sahlins and co-authors (1996) who use the term "the sadness of sweetness" to refer to philosophical, Christian, and psychoanalytic perceptions of the pleasure-pain principle as they bear on "the *triste trope* in Western thinking that what life is all about is the search for satisfaction" (395). Sweetness is sad because "anyone who defines life as the pursuit of happiness must be chronically unhappy" (415). Examined below is another example, João Biehl's book *Vita* (2005), which deploys a deep focus on individual experience in a single life story as a means to contextualize suffering.

Languages of Suffering

Vita is a place for ex-humans. I use this concept reluctantly as I try to express the difficult truth that these persons have been de facto terminally excluded from what counts as reality. I first thought of the term "ex-human" as Catarina told me, "I am an ex," and constantly referred to herself as an "ex-wife" and her kin as "my ex-family." It is not that the souls in Vita have had their humanity and personhood drawn out and are now left without the capacity to understand, to dialogue, and to keep struggling. Rather, when I say ex-human, I want to highlight the fact that these people's efforts to constitute their lives vis à vis institutions meant to confirm and advance humanness were deemed good for nothing and that their supposed inhumanness played an important role in justifying abandonment. João Biehl, *Vita* (2005: 52)

Vita centers on the life of one woman, Catarina, a rural worker and young bride who migrates to the state capital Porto Alegre in Brazil to seek work in the shoe industry. Over time Catarina began to experience persistent physical pain. She gradually became unable to work and slowly fell victim to Brazil's economic decline. Over the next few years she was admitted to different mental institutions and variously diagnosed with schizophrenia, psychosis, anxiety, and depression. She finally ended up on the edges of Porte Alegre in Vita, which Biehl (2005) describes as an institutionalized "zone of social abandonment," or a dumping ground, where society's unwanted, mentally ill, homeless, and unemployed are left to die (20). Biehl addresses what he calls the humanity of Catarina's suffering through her life story and the words in the "dictionary" that she is compiling as a way to record her experiences. In doing so, he tells a larger story about the integral role places like Vita play in poor households, city life, and "ways social processes affect the course of biology and of dying" (8). Catarina's subjectivity and her words are the channel through which Biehl unfolds how her "abnormality" and exclusion are solidified through others' deliberations over her mental state and make her life practically impossible. Vita is a place where individuals no longer considered people wait both for and "*with* death" (1). In her words, in Vita, Catarina feels "dead alive, dead outside, alive inside" (8).

Drawing from anthropology, psychiatry, cultural history, and psychoanalysis, Biehl (2005) shows us how Vita's occupants and its staff become caught in the lack of training, funds, and infrastructure; mental disorders; AIDS; tuberculosis; a moral economy of exploitation; and loveless sexual encounters. He follows Catarina as she refuses to accept her forced abandonment, alleged mental illness, and the cruel rejection of her ex-husband, brothers, family, and friends. In a style akin to a mystery thriller, Biehl eventually reveals she has been persistently misdiagnosed and unnecessarily medicated. She is not "mad" at all. Instead, she is suffering from a fatal neurological disorder, Machado–Joseph disease. This hereditary degenerative neurological disease affects people in Brazil of Azorean descent like Catarina. It paralyzes Catarina and leaves her wheelchair-bound. In this state she becomes effectively useless to her family. Unviable, because she is unable to work, she is an "unnecessary component of a migrant and urban poor culture" (247). Catarina finally dies. Although her death is inevitable, it haunts the reader with the futility that no words, neither Biehl's nor Catarina's own, can save her.

Biehl (2005) argues that individual narratives of patients such as Catarina maintain a steadfastness and contextuality despite their caretakers' insistence such narratives are nonsense. They give language to the exclusion they embody, and become spaces in which the destinies and desires of the "ex-human" can be reframed (88). Biehl intricately links patterns of what he terms individual and "social psychosis." He effectively shows his reader how "novel conjunctions of kinship, public institutions, psychiatry and medication work, if not to make people psychotic, then to give a certain form and value to their experience as psychotic, thus recasting intersubjectivity and mediating abandonment" (106).

Vita illuminates the social and deeply personal literal languages of this struggle: "Catarina's writings and her efforts to heal herself enough to be human again evince pain and an ordinary life force seeking to break through forms and foreclosures and define a kind of subjectivity that is as much about swerves and escapes as about determinants" (367). Through Catarina's life story, Biehl develops a "human" critique of the machines of social death in which the unwanted are caught and struggle through words to survive, to be, and to connect with a wider humanity. Catarina expresses this herself when she writes, "I am part of the origins, not just of language, but of people ... I represent the origins of the person" (360).

Vita powerfully shows how single cases may effectively destabilize the language of conventional clinical, social, and political categories. The book received mixed reviews. Isabel Rodrigues (2006: 773) praises Biehl's account of how "human death and suffering is inescapably tied to a Kafkian medical system where layer upon layer of bureaucracy, medical unaccountability and patronizing hierarchies which obscure and obliterate the causal forces that plunge humans in an ex-human existence." Thomas Csordas (2007) deems *Vita* a landmark work on the humanity of suffering. Despite its "aesthetics of misery," "it is nevertheless a sensitive portrait of afflicted people who, despite the tragedy of social abandonment and existential erasure, remain unmistakably human" (2012). Less enthusiastically, Claudia Fonseca (2006) criticizes the way Biehl positions himself as the sole channel for Catarina's voice: "The tone of moral indignation seems to point an accusing finger at just about everyone (state officials, patients' families, hospital and shelter administrators, etc.), leaving 'Catarina's anthropologist' to restore humanity, both metaphorically and materially, where all others have failed" (686). Clara Han (2012), too, is critical, and singles out Biehl's use of the concept "abandonment." She argues he downplays the subtleties of local relationships and the ways local relations do not simply register "market effects" but are also autonomous of larger neoliberal values, and not always perceptible through notions of abandonment. Han provokes us to think of abandonment not as something that "occurs" but as a condition people move in and out of to endure their suffering. She sees this condition distorted in the language of absolute terms like abandonment—despite Biehl's (2005) claim, he takes up Byron Good's challenge to keep the inarticulacy, ambiguities, and unfinishedness of human subjectivity in mental illness in view (18).

Many academics outside anthropology have also chosen the individual life story as a medium to capture the lived experience and social histories of treating mental illness. Some suffer from mental illness themselves, and several use the language of personal memoirs. To give some examples, the

British psychoanalyst Barbara Taylor's book *The Last Asylum* (2014) unsparingly details her time in one of London's last Victorian mental asylums. Elyn Saks's (2008) biography describes her experience as an American lawyer with high-functioning schizophrenia. American lawyer Jim Jones (2011) and psychiatrist Kay Jamison (2011) both published personal memoirs of their experiences with bipolar disorder. These testimonial biographies vividly capture the firsthand experience of suffering and also aim to ameliorate the stigma of others who suffer from mental disorders. This genre of writing also aligns with notable literary examples. For example, Alphonse Daudet's *In the Land of Pain* (2002) recounts in excruciating detail his   **19** struggles with syphilis and the many ineffectual treatments he endured before his death in France in 1897, including those of leading neurologist Jean-Martin Charcot. Sylvia Plath's book *The Bell Jar* was published one month before Plath's suicide in 1963. This account of the hospitalization of a young woman with severe depression has become a literary classic.

Suffering and Time

While biographies describe the relation of suffering to the temporality of the life-course in highly personalized accounts, we might also consider some relations of suffering ideas about time in professional languages. Indeed, professionalized languages about the duration of mental disorder have profound effects on mental illness outcomes and on ideas of recovery (Good et al. 2010). Anthropologists, for example, have leveled strong critiques at the notion of "chronicity," the idea of lifelong disorder, and ways that dependencies on therapeutic and pharmaceutical regimes can transform acute conditions or illness into chronic lifelong experiences of disorder (Manderson and Smith-Morris 2010). Lenore Manderson and Carolyn Smith-Morris (2010) stress the importance of developing theoretical positions on time and space that can contribute to interventions around medicalized categories such as "chronic" and "acute." Luhrmann (2007) links chronic diagnoses and chronic social stresses. She argues that long-term experiences of social defeat may lead to a sensitized vulnerability to schizophrenia and turn a brief psychotic reaction into chronic clienthood by repeatedly creating the conditions for social defeat (146).

In her compelling study in New Mexico, Angela Garcia (2008) criticizes the chronicity model of addiction. Through the story of one woman addict's ("Alma") death by overdose, she criticizes the biomedical construction of addiction as a lifelong incurable "disease." She shows how ideas that addiction is lifelong interact with local, historically informed discourses of "endless suffering" around the dispossession of people's land. In Hispano families, heroin is a medicine that both creates and relieves pain intergenerationally. With its premise of inevitable relapse (return to pain), the chronicity model of addiction effectively undermines people's chances, and their hopes of recovery.

Studies such as Garcia's (2008) highlight ways illegal drugs serve as a powerful panacea for pain and a form of self-medication. Other anthropologists have likewise focused on the temporal dimensions of addiction (Raikhel and Garriott 2013), and on the "anesthetic" desire to prevent pain and the desire to produce pleasure through drug use (Meyers 2013, 2014). Addiction is of course not confined to drug use. Natasha Dow Schüll's (2012) book *Addiction by Design* describes the casino as a sensorial anesthetic space that can also dull our pain, our sense of life, our contempt for others' pleasure, and the impossibility of really understanding another's pain.

Social Suffering

This section now shifts from a singular focus on individual lives to some collective forms and social causes, and particularly work developed around "social suffering." Arthur Kleinman, Veena Das, Margaret Lock, Paul Farmer, Allen Young, and Mamphela Ramphele among others are all originary voices in this tradition. These authors all diversely highlight ways the workings of global political, economic, social, cultural, and institutional power become embodied in physical and psychological states of illness. Broadly, "social suffering" highlights the damage to subjectivity by events ranging from the violence of categorization, extreme political violence, and the "soft knife" of routine oppression (Kleinman, Das, and Lock 1996: xi). It prioritizes ways mental disorders may be collective responses to social forms of violence rather than exclusively individual illness. The tradition additionally criticizes ways that pain, death, and mourning become metamorphosed into bureaucratic responses, diagnoses of individual pathology, and professional languages that may exacerbate the very problems they seek to improve (Kleinman, Das, and Lock 1996: xii).

Social suffering theorists engage a long-standing tradition in anthropology that addresses difficulties with understanding and representing pain in language. Elaine Scarry's book *The Body in Pain: The Making and Unmaking of the World* (1985) offers a radical thesis on the relationship between embodiment, pain, wounding, and imagining. Scarry argues that pain is central, to quote the book's subtitle, to "the making and unmaking of the world." "Intense pain," she writes, "is world-destroying" (29). It is an experience that destroys the world of the subject while resisting or eluding expression in language. Regarded as a classic, Scarry's book continues to influence work in diverse disciplines, as well as discussions in medical science, non-governmental organizations (NGOs), and charities.

In the social suffering tradition, Veena Das (1996) writes about Indian women who are survivors of violence. She draws on the philosophy of

Ludwig Wittgenstein and Stanley Cavell to interrogate the lack of language in social sciences to "gaze at, touch or become textual bodies on which pain is written" (67). She describes the statement "I am in pain" as a claim asking for an acknowledgment that the listener may understand, give, or deny (70). To ignore such a claim is arguably to deny its existence; hence, it is an act of violence (Cavell 1996: 94–95). Das (1996: 95) argues the study of social suffering must analyze society's silence toward it, not mimic the forms of social silence that perpetuate suffering. In her book *Life and Words* (2007a), Das develops the importance of analyzing the silences around words, or what is *not* said, to grasp how suffering is constituted. Rather than analyze speech, the ethnographic task is to give the survivors of violence "voice." This means exploring the everyday for what may be unspoken, or unsaid, for clues that will restore a context of meaning and expression to experiences that have become "frozen, numb, without life" (8).

Das stresses we should acknowledge and study the inchoate aspects of suffering. Taking a different approach, Kleinman (1988a) argues that suffering can be treated as if its inchoate aspects are transformed into narrative form. He presents the idea of "illness narratives" as a means to contextualize subjectivity ("give voice") and to link personal experiences of illness to therapeutic interpretations which are co-constructed between patient and physician. For Kleinman (1988a, 1995), narrativization can be a reflexive, therapeutic, and transformative process where complex and disjointed *lived* experiences of illness become *interpreted* (given structure, moral sense, coherence, and meaning) through dialogue between the person with the illness, medical professionals, and family members. In other words, cultural and biomedical constructions of health and illness, international health policy and health care systems, and the social determinants of mental health may all be positively interwoven in the illness narrative. Yet Kleinman's argument is perhaps idealistic when we consider Biehl's account of how Catarina's social exclusion and inherited illness became so thoroughly recast as the language of mental disorder by professionals and her family that any personal narrative or sense of self was utterly erased, save as fragments in her dictionary. In fact, the social processes that led to Catarina's death caution us not to underestimate how words, when they are translated into realities, may be lethal. Words can kill.

Other writers also highlight relationships of power between professionals, the person with the illness, and languages of interpretation. For Talal Asad (2011), the medical science model subsumes the sufferer's credibility within its requirements for evidence. He queries the way "body and world come to be severed or yoked together in pain" through relations between the "mental" and "physical" (657–58). These relations are often determined accidentally, post hoc, and by practical and institutional concerns. Asad evokes a vivid image of the mind that painfully bears society's structures by forcing the person/body feeling deep pain into a particular interpretation and conviction that they are ill (658). This work highlights the relation between professionalized languages, individual experience, and the transformations of suffering that occur between these two poles.

Jason Throop's (2010) ethnography of the Yap in Micronesia analyzes how pain involves fragmentary and disjunctive, and also coherent and meaningful, types of experience. Throop proposes that physical and psychical pain occur "as poles along a continuum of possibilities, both personally and culturally influenced, to interpret and communicate dysphoric experiences in terms of mental or bodily idioms of distress" (7). The Yap interpret pain experiences as positive, meaningful relational experiences. These serve to cement kin relations, cultural values of suffering, endurance, and ethical self-control. Throop also highlights discrepancies between patient experiences and health care providers who decide if the problem is psychological or social. While interpreting others' pain is fraught with power, it can also enfold a "mutuality of suffering and vulnerability" that can inspire an empathic orientation toward the other, providing anthropologists with a powerful opportunity for ethical action (7).

This is not always straightforward. To what extent should we maintain an empathic orientation when we "humanize" the suffering of people who commit terrible acts? In his essay "Colonial War and Mental Disorder" ([1963] 2001), the psychiatrist Frantz Fanon changed his mind about revolutionary violence as an exalted way for Algeria's colonized subjects to regain humanity. He became increasingly dismayed at the devastation of the mental health of the patients (militants) he saw. As a consequence, Fanon turned against the revolutionary leaders he had previously supported. I have struggled with questions of empathy and the concord between individual and political madness in my own work on militants in Pakistan (Khan 2010, 2016). Perhaps one way to take such stories as an ideal for the "good," as Robbins (2013) asks us, would be to take issue with the ways critics, academics, and media commentators commonly fetishize violence and are enthralled by it, while they condemn it. So how might critiques of power lead to effective intervention, or indeed end up reproducing the very forms of human suffering they protest?

From Critique to Action?

How might we move toward a framework for action? Let us think more about what Robbins' ideal of the "good" might actually mean and implicate in terms of alleviating suffering—as an ideal, as practice, and as a critique of institutional forms of power.

Can the social suffering tradition do any practical "good"? Ian Wilkinson and Arthur Kleinman in their book *A Passion for Society* (2016) argue it can.

They painstakingly develop their argument drawing on debates from intellectual history, moral philosophy, literature, religious ideology and early Christian writings, and through examples of the plague, the Spanish imperial abuses of the Amerindians, Chinese factory work, social reform movements, and natural disasters. Combining approaches from sociology and anthropology, they argue that the role of structural violence in causing and conditioning distress and the social distribution of mental illness demands moral and critical scrutiny. This should be used to advocate for an intellectually grounded, more humane place for social science in social care, and for forging "more adequate responses to suffering" (15).

Addressing the modern sensibility that human misery is deeply interiorized *and* often a collective experience, Wilkinson and Kleinman (2016) trace histories of social science and social care through the eighteenth and nineteenth centuries, when Euro-American thinkers hoped to assist individuals and whole populations caught in desperate conditions, to the 1940s and 1950s when social medicine took health as an important arena for building projects that could improve grinding poverty, displacement, homelessness, chronic mental and physical illness, and violence (viii). These objectives later disappeared in the scientification of professional research and the cynical demands of individual careerism (viii–ix). The authors promote a form of social inquiry that involves a moral commitment to build more humane forms of society. "On our account, it requires the cultivation of a 'humanitarian social imaginary' and a commitment to humanitarian social reform'" (xi). This perspective should also be read as development of a "care perspective" in social science (xi). They discuss the history of critical debate, the "moral feelings aroused by the spectacle of human misery" (20), the cultural limitations of social science as ameliorative practice. They also provide an overview of some practical applications, and emphasize the potential in both the pedagogy of caregiving and in *real* acts of caregiving: "We take this as necessary for the cultivation of sociologies and anthropologies to inspire genuine hope for humanity, and above all, the passion to sustain the care required to deliver this in lived experience" (23). This moral, intellectual, *and* practical treatise constitutes a passionate call to care through deepening social understandings of suffering, and it combines an ideal with a realistic, pragmatic approach to practice.

In terms of the institutional development, delivery, and conceptualization of "care," humanitarianism has provided anthropologists much food for critical thought. Certainly "West helps the rest" ideologies have long saturated stubborn asymmetries and concerns with humanitarianism's deserving subject: from an Orientialist view of regions and nations as permanently underdeveloped to modernist queries about their progressive incorporation into the technological, secularizing, and liberalizing "Western" mission; to regional developments of war, emergency, and disaster, or refugee crises as incidents of circular repetition or descent into chaos. Criticisms also abound of the contradictions inherent in "humanitarianism," the "international humanitarian project," "humanitarian industry," and "humanitarian architecture," and their application in business, bureaucratic, and military agendas (e.g., Apthorpe 2014; De Lauri 2016; Fassin 2011; Fassin and Rechtman 2009). Antonio De Lauri (2016: 1–8) usefully summarizes four of the key criticisms. First, the sympathetic impulse and myth that the best life is the Euro-American one promotes scripts of "saving lives," those in "need," and oversimplistic solutions to "underdevelopment." Second, the large-scale mobilization of "experts" from donor countries to the Global South is tied to the wild-market model of the global economy. Third, humanitarianism as a multibillion-dollar business links to the privatized military industry, infantilizing forms of intervention that elide destruction and development, and Western powers in partnership with high finance, state governance, and geopolitics. Fourth, "humanitarian culturalism" generates moral hierarchies of humanity between those who aid and receive.

This last position is extensively interrogated in Fassin's book *Humanitarian Reason* (2011). Fassin develops a Foucauldian critique of humanitarianism as a tool of domination, power, and governance that institutes the very conditions it opposes. He also criticizes social suffering work for colluding in projects of moral coercion and a repressive cultural politics that only recognizes people insofar as they are victims of some health deprivation (153). Wilkinson and Kleinman (2016) elaborate a detailed response to Fassin. They argue that his wholesale denunciation of writers on social suffering—whom he deems "infected" with humanitarian ideology—fails to recognize their clearly delineated position of "critical pragmatism" and their moral aim to practically balance sympathetic recognition and action with rational analysis (155). Crucially, they say Fassin fails to acknowledge the consequences of his own moral values and criticisms that privilege critique as an end in itself over any practical way of changing social conditions and improving social existence (158). Instead, critique should be a positive, even if practically flawed, modality to reimagine and transform hegemonic orders—particularly of social science practice (160). Social science practice *must* go beyond pure intellectual critique and engage pragmatically with care systems, even if flawed, to transform hegemonic orders and suffering on behalf of our fellow human beings (160). Wilkinson and Kleinman invite us to turn unpredictability, interruption, and violent loss into new opportunities for reflection that work in tandem with (not separately from) new kinds of response. We revisit these critiques in Chapter 4's discussions of trauma, and the urgent "calls to access" pharmaceutical drugs promoted by global mental health advocates are discussed in Chapter 6.

In conclusion, then, critiques centered on suffering and pain have shifted anthropology's focus away from traditional culture concepts toward alternative languages of representing mental illness. They highlight ways individual experiences and explanations may oppose institutionalized knowledge. If we reject professionalized languages to represent the ideal of the "humanity" of the suffering subject, we risk rejecting scientific advances that can ameliorate people's suffering, or achieving Robbins's "anthropology of the good." Better, following Wilkinson and Kleinman, to think about how good social science can create good social care. In short, while "culture" has been replaced with newer forms of analysis, the culture concept still remains useful to analyses of mental disorder. It is its specific uses that imply too much 25 coherence and unity of belief and practice in particular communities that are problematic. Finally, the essentializing nature of the "suffering subject" paradigm itself may de-emphasize the fact people do *not* suffer all the time. Many psychiatric circles have engaged positive mental states related to human flourishing in counterpoint to the negative. This approach is sometimes known as positive psychology. Chapter 3 develops these discussions in relation to ways culture has been deployed in the history of contemporary psychiatry.

Discussion and Activities

Conduct an analysis based on an individual or a first-person account of mental illness as found in an ethnography, autobiography, film, or documentary. What features distinguish these modes of representation? What cultural tropes underpin narratives of mental illness?

Write a short personal illness narrative. (You do not need to share this.) Reflect on the act of writing. In what way does it revive, transform, edit, or otherwise engage biographical memory? How is your narrative, and understanding of your experience, influenced by where you envisage yourself in your life course?

"Life can only be understood backwards, but it must be lived forwards." Discuss the relevance of this quote by the philosopher Kierkegaard for analyzing personal narratives of mental illness.

Compose a short summary on intellectual approaches to pain. What is the usefulness, and what are the problems in conceptualizing pain as cultural?

How is mental disorder constructed, contested, and transformed through language?

Additional Films and Readings

Films

Family Victim. 2010. Directed by Robert Lemelson. Afflictions: Culture and Mental Illness in Indonesia. Anthropology and Psychiatry Film Series. Watertown, MA: Documentary Educational Resources.

Standing on the Edge of a Thorn. 2012. Directed by Robert Lemelson. Afflictions: Culture and Mental Illness in Indonesia. Anthropology and Psychiatry Film Series. Watertown, MA: Documentary Educational Resources.

Readings

Das, Veena. 2007. *Life and Words: Violence and the Descent into the Ordinary*. Berkeley: University of California Press.

Das, Veena. 2015. *Affliction: Health, Disease, Poverty*. Bronx, NY: Fordham University Press.

Eggerman, Mark, and Catherine Panter-Brick. 2010. "Suffering, Hope, and Entrapment: Resilience and Cultural Values in Afghanistan." *Social Science & Medicine* 71: 71–83.

Good, Byron, J. Subandi, and Mary-Jo DelVecchio Good. "The Subject of Mental Illness: Psychosis, Mad Violence and Subjectivity in Indonesia." In *Subjectivity: Ethnographic Investigations*, edited by João Biehl, Byron Good, and Arthur Kleinman, 243–72. Berkeley: University of California Press.

Hurwitz, Brian, Trisha Greenhalgh, and Vieda Skultans, eds. 2004. *Narrative Research in Health and Illness*. Oxford: Blackwell.

Littlewood, Roland. 2002. *Pathologies of the West. An Anthropology of Mental Illness in Europe and America*. Ithaca, NY: Cornell University Press.

Raikhel, Eugene, and William Garriot, eds. 2013. *Addiction Trajectories*. Durham, NC: Duke University Press.

Skultans, Vieda. 2011. *Empathy and Healing: Essays in Medical and Narrative Anthropology*. New York: Berghahn Books.

Valentine, Daniel, E. 1996. "Crushed Glass, or Is There a Counterpoint to Culture?" In *Culture/Contexture: Explorations in Anthropology and Literary Studies*, edited by Daniel E. Valentine and Jeffrey Peck, 357–75. Berkeley: University of California Press.

26

CHAPTER 3

CULTURE, PSYCHIATRY, AND CULTURES
OF PSYCHIATRY

In particular, the relative absence of delusions amongst the Javanese might be related to the lower stage of intellectual development attained, and the rarity of auditory hallucinations might reflect the fact that speech counts for far less than it does with us and that thoughts tend to be governed more by sensory images.
—Emil Kraepelin, "Comparative Psychiatry" ([1904] 2000)

This discussion examines the origins of cultural psychiatry in colonialism, colonialism's legacy in contemporary psychiatry, and the development of "culture-bound syndromes." Rather than provide a full review of the extensive statistical clinical information about these disorders, the focus is on developing useful ways to interpret them. It explores the relevance of anthropological thinking to wider developments around cultural diversity, cultural psychiatry, and culturally informed treatments. Culture refers here, in its broadest sense, to the cultural assumptions that underpin the "psych" and mental health professions. This raises for us some key questions. What challenges does anthropology make to colonialist under-standings of culture and psychiatric illness? How do patterns recognized as a mental disorder occur at particular cultural and historical moments? How can anthropologists assist mental health professionals working with minorities, marginalized communities, or "indigenous" people, especially where recognized oppression and mental illness are brought to the fore via ideas of pathologized culture—and Western societies are generally seen as "culture-free"? What can anthropology contribute to problems of conceptual translation and elements of psychiatric classifications that may be generally applicable, or else culturally specific?

Culture, Psychiatry, and Colonialism

The history of cultural psychiatry can be summarized into three trends. First is the period of comparative psychiatry associated with the earliest global explorations, when European fleets set sail to discover and conquer the world. Declaring everything they discovered as theirs, which, Kirmayer (2013) observes in his online lecture "Cultural Psychiatry: A Critical Introduction," is an arguably psychotic characteristic itself, the British, French, and Spanish established empires through violent means during the imperial wars. In the 1500s the Spanish court debated whether natives in the Americas deserved treatment as full humans, according to Catholic theology, or whether they posed an offense to "natural law," which justified enslaving, killing, and brutalizing them. Second, in the colonial phase (mostly the 1600s and 1700s), people moved from the European metropoles to the colonies, and profited from the resources and the people they found. They built institutions to govern, including institutions of social welfare and social control, such as asylums for the "insane." These asylums provided the laboratories for early studies in comparative psychiatry. German psychiatrist Emil Kraepelin became interested in questions of universality and cross-cultural variation. He traveled to an asylum in Indonesia where he observed patients. He concluded that similarities between European and Indonesian patients outweighed any differences. Rather, he attributed the differences he found, for example in the content of delusions, to racialized causes such as intellectual inferiority. Third, the age of colonial expansion introduced a style of explanation of racialized hierarchies in which white people emerged as superior, more civilized, and mature. This idea of essential characteristics underpinned by race became attached to cultural systems and colonial psychiatry. For example, Antoine Porot was a founder of the influential "Algiers School" of colonial psychiatry in North Africa in the late 1800s. Colonial psychiatrists here drew on stereotypes of North Africans as lazy, duplicitous, dishonest criminals. Not speaking the local languages, they could not understand the cultures they were investigating in any depth. Moreover, they examined only the severely ill and, extrapolating from descriptions of the most florid psychotic behaviors, applied these to whole cultures (Kirmayer 2013).

The European exoticization of the native or colonized subject is endemic to the history of both colonial psychiatry and colonial asylums. Edgar and Sapire (2000: 34) suggest the confinement of mad Africans was less about "curing" or alleviating their mental suffering than removing them as sources of disturbance to society. Others argue colonial psychiatry was more complicated than its critics suggest. Richard Keller (2007: 4) highlights ways the discipline served as a tool for the emancipation of the colonized and as an innovative branch of social and medical science. Vaughan (1991) argues that the colonial asylum points to the limits of racial ideologies of difference. That is, far from standing for the savage Other, the madness of colonial subjects was feared because it broke the barriers of difference constructed around culture. It was "deculturating": it was individuals who had "forgotten" who they were and had stopped conforming to the notion of the African subject who were most often incarcerated (Vaughan 1991: 118). Many forms of difference constructed between black and white were also threatened by insanity. The suffering of the black insane signaled not their barbarism but their humanity (Parle 2007). Likewise, the white insane who degenerated into alcoholism, transgressive and careless sexually **29** behavior, and irrationality demonstrably failed to *maintain* the levels of civilized behavior that should distinguish white from black: insufficiently Other, the white insane had "gone native" (Parle 2007: 19).

Nonetheless, a generation of "African psychiatry" provided "evidence" of defective brains (Carothers 1951; McCulloch 2006). The desire of the African to free himself from French colonialist rule was seen as evidence of a mental disorder and a "fact" taught in French universities until, incredibly, the 1960s (Fanon [1963] 2001). Scientific racism, we have discussed, dominated the early twentieth century with its biological determinism, comparative anatomy, and classificatory systems based on racial "types" and "native minds." In 1973 cultural anthropologist Raphael Patai first published *The Arab Mind*, advocating a tribal-group-survival explanation of Arab "culture." Just preceding the US-led war in Iraq in 2002, an updated reprint was published with new information about the proud and ancient Arab culture, the Arabs' tendency toward extremes of behavior, their intense concern with honor and courage, and their ambivalent attitudes toward the West. These kinds of Orientalist stereotypes have persisted largely uncritically and with incredible force in the post–9/11 contexts of fears of violent Islamic extremism and global terrorism.

These are good examples that demonstrate how the assumption that we even know *what* the key mental disorders are, developed through the Western intellectual tendency, exaggerates people's similarities or differences via notions of pathology (and proposes pathology's apparent resolution in therapy) (Littlewood 2002: xiii). Despite efforts to develop a more interactional view, many colonial traces prevail. Echoing Kraepelin's ([1904] 2000) view, Western psychiatry still considers somatization (the physical symptomology of mental suffering, more likely in cultures that de-emphasize the verbal articulation of emotion) as primitive when compared with psychologization, a supposedly more mature expression (Kirmayer 1986).

Next, let us turn to ways culture has been dealt with in official psychiatric nosology in the formulation of "culture-bound syndromes." The term, first developed by Pow Ming Yap in 1969, delineated a rare and exotic group of disorders consisting of unpredictable and chaotic behavior. Our first critique concerns how anthropologists' studies of these disorders have done much to rework colonial notions of culture.

Culture-bound Syndromes

The publication of the DSM-IV (APA 1994, 898–901) included an appendix containing a glossary of 25 culture-bound and culture-related syndromes. It defines culture-bound syndromes as "recurrent, locality-specific repetitive patterns of behavior and troubling experience, indigenously considered to be illnesses with a local name that may or may not be linked to a DSM-IV diagnostic category." The 25 DSM-IV culture-bound syndromes have their counterpart in the ICD-10. They are listed here with their principal places of origin: *Amok* (Malaysia, Indonesia, Philippines, Brunei, Singapore), *ataque de nervios* (Hispanic people, Philippines), *bilis/cólera* (Latinos), *bouffée délirante* (West Africa, Haiti), brain fag (West Africa), *dhat* (India), falling out (Southern United States, Caribbean), ghost sickness (Native American), *hwa-byeong* (Korea), *koro* (Southeast Asia, Chinese and Malay populations), *latah* (Malaysia, Indonesia), *locura* (Latinos in the United States and Latin America), evil eye (Mediterranean, Ethiopia, Hispanic populations), *nervios* (Latinos), *pibloktoq* (Eskimo populations, Arctic, subartic), *qi-gong* psychotic reaction (Chinese), rootwork (Southern US, Caribbean), *sangue dormido* (Portuguese in Cape Verde), *shenjing shuairuo* (Chinese), *shenkui* (Chinese), *shin-byeong* (Korean), spell (Southern United States, Ethiopia), *susto* (Latinos in the United States, Mexico, and Central and South America), *taijin kyofusho* (Japan), and *zar* (Ethiopia, Somalia, Egypt, Sudan, Iran, North Africa, and the Middle East).

Whereas physicians typically emphasize the universal neuropsychological dimensions of culture-bound phenomena, anthropologists argue they should be investigated on their own terms (Guarnaccia and Rogler 1999). Criticisms concern the appendix's disconnection from the main DSM text as a sort of exotic "cabinet of curiosities" and adjunct to mainstream medicine's more serious concerns, whether these phenomena describe syndromes at all, and whether the term "syndrome" detracts from the violence of the colonial and postcolonial encounter by emphasizing causal explanations. Let us examine some examples.

First we might look at *latah*, found in Indonesia and Malaysia. *Latah* describes a person who is startled, freezes, then is compelled to imitate another person, curse, or behave with impropriety. The syndrome was "discovered" by the anthropologist-psychiatrist Ronald Simons (1980, 1983, 1996) who frames *latah* as a cultural elaboration of the startle reflex. *Latah*, he argues, can be created by repeatedly startling someone, and may also be deployed as a source of village entertainment. Even the person being startled may derive pleasure from *latah*, which sanctions and controls behavior typically taboo in Malay village culture. Reflecting on Simons's conclusions, Baer, Clark, and Peterson (1998: 185) argue it is unclear if Simons is describing a cathartic social function or a symbol of marginality rather than a culture-specific psychiatric illness requiring treatment.

Second, *amok* (sudden mass assault) describes a putatively rare culture-bound syndrome (Burton-Bradley 1985; Horowitz 2002; Littlewood 2002; Williamson 2010). It was originally observed about two centuries ago in remote island populations around Malaysia, Indonesia, and the Philippines. *Amok* describes the situation whereupon an individual who felt humiliated might brood for days then suddenly run wild and kill many people, with no recollection of his or her actions afterwards. The classification of *amok* in the DSM-IV, according to specificities from colonial times, perpetuates many ideas of primitivism and tribalism that characterized colonial attitudes. It also discourages an examination of ways cultural beliefs (violent redress, heroism, defense of honor) may interact with contemporary understandings of psychosis, personality pathology, and psychosocial stressors, including early contacts with colonizers (Horwitz 2002: 105).

Koro occurs in China and Southeast Asia. *Koro* refers to the fear of fatal genital retraction (Edwards 1985; Lin, Kleinman, and Lin 1980). The onset of *koro* is rapid and intense, and it can present as a mass hysteria event or panic, as for example when an epidemic among Chinese men occurred in Singapore in 1967. This particular event followed in the wake of independence from the British in 1963, which involved the British ejection or separation from Malaysia, the deadly race riots between Chinese and Malays in 1964, and the massive widespread anti-Communist killings in neighboring Indonesia in 1965. The ethnicized nature of fears involving (noncircumcised) Chinese and (circumcised) Muslim Malays would also suggest further investigation, yet these are relatively unelaborated connections in analyses of the epidemic.

An interesting example that further highlights some disturbing processes by which an exploitative, abusive encounter between two peoples became transformed into a culture-bound syndrome is *pibloktoq*. *Pibloktoq*, a polar Inuit term referred to in the DSM as "Arctic hysteria," describes a situation where a person becomes very agitated, strips off their clothes, runs across the freezing tundra, may roll on the ground and eat feces, and if not restrained will die of exposure. *Pibloktoq* is attributed with precise, scientific criteria— for example, as lasting from 30 minutes up to 12 hours. Anthropologists have proposed various causes, including an excessive consumption of polar bear liver, and a lack of sunlight and vitamin D. Canadian historian Lyle Dick (1995, 2002) collected all the primary descriptions available for *pibloktoq*. He discovered 25 cases in total, all concerning women, and mostly dating from the American explorer Robert Peary's explorations to Greenland in the 1880s. These typically comprised dramatic descriptions such as:

"The mistress of the remaining igloo was making an awful noise and trying to come out of her habitation, while a man was holding her back and talking to her, but she screamed and struggled so long as we remained where she could see us. I asked Mane what was the nature of the trouble and he told me the woman was pi-bloc-toc (mad)" (Dick 1995: 3).

Dick (1995) discovered in his investigations that when Peary set out with the Inuit men to map the land, he left his sailors behind with the women. Plied with alcohol and sexually exploited, some women went *pibloktoq*. Dick concludes that *pibloktoq* was a repository for explorers to conjoin various Inuit anxiety reactions, symptoms of physical (and staged) illness, expressions of resistance to patriarchy, sexual coercion, and shamanistic practice, many of which were induced by the stresses of early contact between Euro-Americans and Inuit between 1890 and 1920 (23).

Culture-related or Culture-bound?

Not all critiques of culture-bound syndromes are directed at practices of colonialism. Others raise concerns about the classification of culture in psychiatry. We have been discussing culture-bound syndromes, in the sense of a set of simultaneously co-existing symptoms that underpin a disorder or illness. However, some phenomena and conditions are arguably so heterogeneous, for example *mal de ojo* (evil eye), they defy DSM categorization altogether (Cummings 2013). *Susto*, occurring across Central and South America, refers to any frightening experience at all, and it may be a common explanation for many problems. *Susto* may therefore better describe a folk illness, or a category, recognized in a culture or an ethnic group by lay people or nonmedical healers, which may or may not be a syndrome or have an explicit explanatory model attached.

Critics of the DSM-IV proposed modifying psychiatric terminology to reflect ways such phenomena may be culture-*related*, or cultural, but not culture-bound. For example, *taijin kyofusho* describes a "culturally distinctive phobia in Japan." It relates to the fear that one's public performance will make others uncomfortable. Yet, depending on the content of the patients' fears that they will publicly displease or embarrass others, *taijin kyofusho* might reasonably be included in the DSM-IV category of social phobia. To give another example, *tajin kyofusho* may also fulfill the criteria for body dysmorphic disorder (Suzuki et al. 2003, who use this alternate spelling of *tajin*). Nor are social fears necessarily pathological. Tajan (2013) suggests that in Japan, *hikikomori* (social withdrawal) more aptly describes a social issue, not an individual pathology.

The term culture-bound also makes many conditions seem highly localized and confined. Many phenomena might better describe cultural syndromes, or "idioms of distress," that reflect common languages of communicating "suffering" rather than a coherent collection of syndromes (Nichter 2010; Kirmayer and Young 1998). Many culture-bound syndromes listed in the DSM-IV also have somatic symptoms, and they might be viewed as forms of somatization (e.g., *bilis* or *coléra*, *hwa-byung*, brain fag, *dhat*, *shenkui*, falling out, *koro*, *shenjing shuairuo*, and neurasthenia) (Gureje et al. 1997; Kirmayer 1984, 1986; Kirmayer and Robbins 1991; Kirmayer and Young 1998). Therefore, it is important to examine how somatic symptoms co-occur with emotional distress, psychosocial stressors, and local languages of expression. For example, in India, *dhat* describes the common belief that losing semen through nocturnal emission, urine, or masturbation depletes vital energy. Yet *dhat* does not always describe the physical symptoms of a psychiatric disorder. It can also function as a common explanation for feeling run down (Kirmayer and Young 1998; Mehta, De, and Balachandran 2009). Similarly, depression links to the symptoms of a major clinical disorder, but the saying "I'm depressed" is also just an everyday way of communicating distress. **33**

How do culture-bound syndromes relate to DSM diagnoses? How do they travel across cultures? Let us take *ataque de nervios*, one of the best researched culture-bound syndromes, found among Latino populations. *Ataque de nervios* is also an idiom of distress: while symptoms may be syndromic, they do not always represent psychopathology (Guarnaccia, Lewis-Fernández et al. 2010). *Ataque* is prominent among Latinos from the Caribbean, Puerto Rico, and Dominican Republic. Its symptoms include shouting uncontrollably, attacks of crying, trembling, becoming verbally or physically aggressive, and a sense of being out of control (Guarnaccia, Lewis-Fernández et al. 2010: 299). Dissociative experiences, seizure-like or fainting episodes, and suicidal gestures also occur. Other symptoms include "intense emotional upset, including acute anxiety, anger, or grief ... and heat in the chest rising into the head" (Lewis-Fernández quoted in Cummings 2013: 833). *Ataque* is more common among women with low socio-economic status (SES) backgrounds and with marital problems (Guarnaccia, Canino et al. 1993), and is associated with anxiety, panic, and both affective and dissociative disorders (Lewis-Fernández, Guarnaccia et al. 2002). It functions as a marker for social and psychiatric vulnerability among children and adolescents in Puerto Rico (Guarnaccia, Martinez et al. 2005), and among Puerto Ricans in Puerto Rico and New York City (Lewis-Fernández et al. 2002).

Guarnaccia, Lewis-Fernández et al. (2010) examined *ataques de nervios* in diverse Latino populations in the United States. They found Puerto Ricans reported higher rates of *ataques de nervios* than other Latino groups. They also found that rates were almost double among women and had strong associations with suicidal and psychotic symptom and dissociative tendencies; *ataques de nervios* also occurred at greater rates among US-born citizens than newer arrivals (304). While they had predicted increased rates among Latinos in their countries of origin, due to having closer proximity to cultural influences, their latter finding concurs with high distress levels found among Latinos on the US mainland due to economic and political circumstances, family disruption, and migration (Amaro et al. 2005). *Ataques* also strongly predicted anxiety and depressive disorders, and people's use of mental health services. Large-scale studies such as these also have clinical utility: the robustness of their findings suggests that if a clinician asks about *ataques de nervios*, he or she may find a way into exploring a whole range of clinically significant social, cultural, and psychiatric issues (Guarnaccia, Lewis-Fernández et al. 2010: 305).

Advances to the DSM

Anthropologists, including Yonkers, Lewis-Fernández, Aggarwal, Guarnaccia, Hinton, Cummings, and Kirmayer, have all made prominent advances to cultural aspects in the development and evaluation of the DSM-5 (see Aggarwal, Desilva et al. 2015; Aggarwal, Krishan et al. 2015; Aggarwal, Nicasio et al. 2013; Parnas and Gallagher 2015; Cummings 2013). Lewis-Fernández, Aggarwal, Bäärnheilm, and colleagues (2014) developed the cultural formulation approach in a very productive way, combining anthropological approaches with clinical experience. They discuss how research over two decades addressing problems and inconsistences with the outline for cultural formulation (OCF) finally became operationalized in the DSM-5's cultural formulation interview (CFI). They highlight how the OCF was developed through literature reviews sponsored by the NIMH in 1991–93, reprinted without revision in DSM-IV, and they summarize the literature reviews and analyses of experience with the OCF conducted by the DSM-5 Cross-Cultural Issues Subgroup (DCCIS). The DCCIS comprised international experts in culture and mental health, and was chaired by Roberto Lewis-Fernández and Kimberly Yonkers. It was charged by the DSM-5 Task Force to make recommendations on racial, ethnic, and cultural issues related to risk factors, precipitants, symptom presentations, prevalence, symptom severity, and course of illness, and to critically review the DSM-IV OCF. In reviewing and refining the OCF, its application and use in training programs, and in developing the CFI, Lewis-Fernández, Aggarwal, Bäärnheilm, and colleagues (2014) adopted a person-centered framework—a sort of mini-ethnography—that could privilege the key issues at stake for the person in their illness. The key challenges for the DSM-5, they stressed, would be to provide guidelines for a patient-centered assessment, incorporate elements of cultural identity excluded from the DSM-IV, and account for cultural elements of the relationship between individual and clinician.

Following the DCCIS's investigations, the DSM-5 is now divided into three sections: Section I, Introduction ("DSM-5 Basics"); Section II, "Diagnostic Criteria and Codes"; and Section III, "Emerging Measures and Models." Section III includes a new chapter on cultural formulation, an approach to assessment using the CFI, and a section discussing "Cultural Concepts of Distress." An appendix at the end of the manual includes a "Glossary of Cultural Concepts of Distress" (APA, 2013: 749–59). The term culture-bound syndrome was replaced by three concepts: (1) *cultural syndromes*, (2) *cultural idioms of distress*, and (3) *cultural explanations of distress or perceived causes* (758). Clinicians are now encouraged to investigate cultural factors in combination with social context and individual anomalous experience.

35

The reformulated glossary (833–38) contains nine culture-bound syndromes. Representing "the best-studied concepts of distress around the world," these are *ataque de nervios* (attack of nerves), *dhat* syndrome (semen loss), *khyâl cap* (wind attack), *kufingisisa* (thinking too much), *maladi moun* (human-caused illness), *nervios* (nerves), *shenjing shuairuo* (re-glossed as weakness of the nervous system), *susto* (fright), and *taijin kyofusho* (interpersonal fear disorder). The glossary also cross-references related conditions in other cultural contexts and in the main DSM-5 text. Lewis-Fernández (quoted in Cummings 2013) illustrates how, for example, *ataque de nervios* in the glossary now cross-references related conditions in other cultural contexts and the main DSM-5 text (e.g., panic disorder). Conversely, a section in the entry under "panic disorder" in Section II: "Culture-Related Diagnostic Issues" (211–12) describes *ataque*, and it refers the reader to the glossary. This new form of cross-referencing, Lewis-Fernández argues, should help practitioners assess each illness in its own right and cultural context, avoid misdiagnosis, obtain clinically useful information, improve clinical rapport and therapeutic efficacy, and clarify cultural epidemiology.

This work by anthropologists has directly and practically changed aspects of culture in relation to the DSM. Other interesting cultural analyses by anthropologists have challenged hegemonic portrayals of individual pathology. For example, Devon Hinton and Byron Good's edited collection, *Culture and Panic Disorder* (2009), critiques dominant understandings of panic attacks through the natural disease model. The authors set out to analyze ways "culture is enormously significant in shaping which bodily sensations or internal experiences may be considered threatening or potentially catastrophic in these societies" (23). Laurence Kirmayer and Caminee Blake's chapter locates panic disorder in geographically and culturally mediated thoughts of catastrophe (31). In their chapter, Hinton and Good take sensations (dizziness, asphyxia, and palpitations) as local, somatic forms of experience that are interpreted through "sensation semiosis" (74). Robert Kugelman explores irritable heart syndrome in the American Civil War as a metaphor for soldiers who experienced their hearts as both mechanical pumps and seats of courage (107).

"Culture-free" Societies

Psychiatry has produced an extraordinary literature on other societies, wherein it has conceived of illnesses as singularly "cultural" but at the same time has avoided attributing cultural significance to disorders in Western societies (Littlewood 2002: xiii). This reflects the ethnocentric discussion in Chapter 1 regarding culture as something only "other people" from non-Western, non-Euro-American societies have. Nonetheless, it is the case that several Western disorders pose eligible candidates. Historically, England in the 1500s was described by Italian physicians as a place liable to *morbus anglicus* (despair and suicide) due to its wet climate, beef diet, fast commercial life, and melancholic national character (Littlewood 2002: 2). Let us briefly consider some further examples.

Anorexia nervosa, for example, is *not* a culture-bound syndrome, although eating disorders occur more in societies where negative concerns with excessive consumption, body fat, body image, and body weight are prevalent (see Kirmayer 2013). Why, therefore, is it not? Next, dependent personality disorder involves excessive dependency and loss of autonomy. Yet it is only viewed as a problem if it is constructed in relation to culturally normative ideas of individualism in Western societies where excessive independence is not problematic. And possession experiences are so common across the world they may be universal. In secular societies where gods or supernatural forces are not available to occupy people, could we think of possession by different fragments of one's own personality describing a similar phenomenon, or expressing a fragmented sense of self (Littlewood 2002: xv)? Such explanations were given for the US epidemic of multiple personality disorder in the 1980s (renamed dissociative identity disorder in the DSM-IV). Yet although dissociative identity disorder is not a culture-bound syndrome, broadened criteria for the DSM-5 have led to the inclusion of possession-form phenomena (Wen-Shing and Strelzer 2013). Despite these "advances," in many societies possession is *not* an illness but a healing practice. Moreover, to the extent *any* abnormal experience may be understood as an external intrusion of another power, might not all mental disorder be viewed as a kind of possession (Littlewood 2002: xiv–xv)? Last, anger and related violence are often cited as a problem in the US. Although the DSM includes many anger-related disorders (temper dysregulation disorder, intermittent explosive disorder, oppositional–defiant disorder, antisocial personality disorder, borderline personality disorder), its structural groupings are organized around anxiety, trauma, and dissociation, not anger specifically. Further, the DSM-5 grouping "Disruptive, impulse-control, and conduct disorders" contains several disorders with high expressed anger, but not every disorder with significant anger components. Might this constitute a cultural blindspot by US psychiatrists (Kirmayer 2013)?

While culture-bound syndromes are localized folk diagnostic categories limited to specific societies, they are also culturally influenced. Many interpretations of disorder are gendered, and powerful images of femininity, sexuality, and motherhood run through many disorders (Appignanesi 2008). Yet we should not reduce every pattern to a singular set of cultural constraints. Littlewood (2002) writes, "A woman's place may certainly be in the home but agoraphobia is not just a gendered prison; men too may **37** become agoraphobic" (xiv). Nor are some feminist interpretations of causality necessarily always the best way to make sense of certain conditions affecting women disproportionately.

Consider the high rates of borderline personality disorder (BPD) diagnosed among women (Lester 2013a). The DSM-5 characterizes BPD in terms of excessive fears of abandonment, feelings of emptiness, the alternate idealization or demonization of significant others, an unstable self, impulsivity, suicidality, mood swings, overwhelming anger, and stress-related paranoia or dissociation (APA 2013). Lester (2013a) takes issue with feminist analysts who attribute high rates of diagnosis among women to historically constructed "feminine" dispositions—such as emotionality, dependency, and instability—and who label these women's casual sexual activity as impulsive and their extreme responses to abandonment as irrational. Rather, experiences of abandonment, invalidation, neglectful or indifferent caregivers, violence, and early sexual abuse *do* affect women disproportionately. BPD may even describe a "brilliant" survival strategy when the woman patient, viewed by clinicians as manipulative and by academics as a construct of psychiatric discourse, is "caught in a paradox of existence where to 'be' in any form renders her inauthentic in a world where her struggles to be heard, form relationships and connect with others are overwhelmingly human" (75–76). The problem is not overdiagnosis, then, but a need to change society's attitudes toward women with BPD, and for mental health professionals to recognize BPD's social and cultural etiology.

To conclude, anthropologists have sought to rid cultural psychiatry of the legacy of colonialism. They have contributed many understandings that can assist clinicians in recognizing clusters or symptoms found in a specific culture or context, syndromes that may not be recognized in the culture, or syndromes that are labeled differently but still occur. The cultural aspect of the DSM-5 now signifies a richer appreciation of the complex interplay of cultural, social, and individual factors in the diagnosis and treatment of psychiatric disorders. Anthropologists provide a useful practical resource for professionals dealing with increasing hyperdiversity resulting from demographic changes, especially in the world's largest cities. Future revisions to psychiatric nosology should evolve with practitioners' expertise, advances in social and cultural epidemiology, individuals' understandings of their illnesses, and changes in cultural variation in ways that psychopathological experiences are constructed (Kirmayer and Ban 2013). We need to develop more diverse forms of nuanced cultural analysis to keep in view the essential ambiguity in ways that illness is shaped by multiple influences, active agency, personal decisions, and experience (Littlewood 2002: xii). Future directions might usefully integrate new theories from cultural psychiatry, philosophy and phenomenology, neuroscience, and anthropology to continue the careful scrutiny of how mental health problems emerge in specific contexts (Kirmayer, Lemelson, and Cummings 2015).

Discussion and Activities

Conduct a cultural analysis of a single disorder. Historical options include drapetomania, fugue, nymphomania, homosexuality, hysteria, melancholia, kleptomania, monomania, neurasthenia, dementia praecox, and dypsomania. Contemporary options include anti-social personality disorder, oppositional defiant disorder, intermittent explosive disorder, premenstrual dysphoric disorder, transvestic fetishism, gender dysphoric disorder, paraphilia, pedophilia, relational disorder, and hoarding.

Conduct an analysis of a culture-bound syndrome from the DSM, developing the historical, political, social, or postcolonial contexts of meaning and influence in your explanation. What factors influence its emergence or disappearance?

To what extent does the conceptual basis of "culture-bound syndromes" rest in the ideology of colonialism? Discuss.

Analyze a "not yet" or emergent disorder that may fit the criteria for a disorder; for example, sluggish cognitive tempo disorder. Alternatively, analyze the reasons a disorder was either dropped or "failed" to be included in the DSM; for example, self-defeating personality disorder, Internet addiction disorder, or masochistic personality disorder.

Research and analyze representations of patients' experiences in an asylum using archival data, photographs, film, or literature. Possible data sources include the Wellcome Library's digitized records, photographs from the Magnum news agency, Shakhnazarov's film *Ward No. 6*, and Doris Lessing's *Briefing for a Descent into Hell*. You may use ideas from colonial and postcolonial theory, feminism, or cultural psychiatry to inform your analysis.

Additional Film and Readings

Film
Mujeres al Borde de un Ataque de Nervios. 1988. Directed by Pedro Almodóvar. Barcelona: Laurenfilm SA.

Readings

Fanon, Frantz. [1963] 2001. "Colonial Wars and Mental Disorders." In *The Wretched of the Earth*. Translated by Constance Farrington, 200–50. London: Penguin.

Gold, Steve. 1994. "Fight Club: A Depiction of Contemporary Society as Dissociogenic." *Journal of Trauma and Dissociation* 5: 13–24.

Hinton, Ladson, Neil Aggarwal, Ana-Maria Iosif, Mitchell Weiss, Vasudeo Paralikar, Smita Deshpande, Sushrut Jadhav, David Ndetei, Andel Nicasio, Marit Boiler, Peter Lam, Yesi Avelar, and Roberto Lewis-Fernández. 2015. "Perspectives of Family Members Participating in Cultural Assessment of Psychiatric Disorders: Findings from the DSM-5 International Field Trial." *International Review of Psychiatry* 1: 3–10.

Hughes, Charles, and Ronald Simons, eds. 1985. *The Culture-Bound Syndromes*. New York: Springer.

Kaiser, Bonnie, and Kristen McLean. 2015. "'Thinking Too Much' in the Central Plateau: An Apprenticeship Approach to Treating Local Distress in Haiti." In *Global Mental Health: Anthropological Perspectives*, edited by Brandon Kohrt and Emily Mendenhall, 277–90. Walnut Creek, CA: Left Coast Press.

Kirmayer, Laurence, Robert Lemelson, and Constance Cummings. 2015. *Re-Visioning Psychiatry: Cultural Phenomenology, Critical Neuroscience, and Global Mental Health*. Cambridge: Cambridge University Press.

Kleinman, Arthur, and Byron Good, eds. 1985. *Culture and Depression: Studies in the Anthropology and Cross-Cultural Psychiatry of Affect and Disorder*. Berkeley: University of California Press.

Lewis-Fernández, Roberto, Neil Krishan Aggarwal, Sofie Bäärnhielm, Hans Rohlof, Laurence J. Kirmayer, Mitchell G. Weiss, Sushrut Jadhav, Ladson Hinton, Renato D. Alarcón, Dinesh Bhugra, Simon Groen, Rob van Dijk, Adil Qureshi, Francisco Collazos, Cécile Rousseau, Luis Caballero, Mar Ramos, and Francis Lu. 2014. "Culture and Psychiatric Evaluation: Operationalizing Cultural Formulation for DSM-5." *Psychiatry* 77: 130–54.

Orr, Jackie. 2006. *Panic Diaries: A Genealogy of Panic Disorder*. Durham, NC: Duke University Press.

Simons, Ronald, and Charles C. Hughes. 1985. *The Culture-Bound Syndromes: Folk Illnesses of Psychiatric and Anthropological Interest*. Dordrecht: Reidel Publishing.

Waldram, James. 2004. *Revenge of the Windigo: The Construction of the Mind and Mental Health of North American Aboriginal Peoples*. Toronto: University of Toronto Press.

Willen, Sarah, with Anne Kohler. 2015. "Cultural Competence and Its Discontents: Reflections on a Mandatory Course for Psychiatry Residents." In *Global Mental Health: Anthropological Perspectives*, edited by Brandon Kohrt and Emily Mendenhall, 239–54. Walnut Creek, CA: Left Coast Press.

CHAPTER 4

THE POLITICS OF TRAUMA

The exact spot where Shelly fell today, pulled to her death, hill to one side, sheer drop to the other. I fell toward the hill, fighting tentacles wrapped round my ankles and wrists. Heathen spirits cackled, mocking my crucifix. These spirits follow whims, not my will. Wish I could trade with Shelly. The two boys need their mother.

—Renato Rosaldo, *The Day of Shelly's Death* (2014, 8)

Anthropologists have found much value in trauma for understanding events that push people to the edges of their existence, in the process of what Scarry (1985) calls "unmaking and remaking worlds." Through events that untie, distort, and rend people, often irreparably, from the bonds that attach them to the everyday world, anthropologists have shown how people are radically or irreversibly transformed (Crapanzano 1985; Lévi-Strauss 1963; Rosaldo 1980, 2014; Young 1995, 2002). Rosaldo's (2014) haunting account of the death of his wife during fieldwork in the Philippines in 1981, from which I quote above, uses "ethnographic poetry" to capture the traumatic shock of "a harrowing experience, the moment of devastating loss, the personal realization of mortality" (102). This volume adds poignancy to Rosaldo's earlier (1980) classic study of Ilongot headhunting, in which he traces how powerful emotions of rage and grief are transformed into bloodlust and the deep enjoyment of taking a head.

This chapter queries the value of some diverse anthropological insights into trauma, healing, and therapeutic processes. It traces these insights from early Freudian ideas of war neurosis, through the emphasis on cultural variation up to the 1980s, through the 1990s onwards when studies of traumatic illness and subjectivity challenged anthropologists to reconceptualize political, legal, and medical spaces of power. This focus concerns the cross-cultural relevance of local variations for clinical practice, and ways trauma operates as a political category in the governance of war, state borders, international law, humanitarianism, and policies around migration. Through such readings, this chapter maps ways anthropologists have expanded the classic fields of medical and psychiatric anthropology in relation to war, exile, chronic poverty, childhood abuses, colonial oppression, and the crisis conditions of contemporary capitalism.

Cultural Variation and Local Responses

In medical terms, trauma describes a physical injury to the body or brain. In psychological terms, it describes individual or collective responses to an event, or prolonged exposure to stressful or violent events. The clinical category of post-traumatic stress disorder was first incorporated into the DSM-III (APA 1980). The DSM-5 defines PTSD in terms of exposure to actual or threatened death, serious injury, or sexual violation. The individual should directly experience the traumatic event, witness it personally, or learn it occurred to a relative or close friend. The DSM-5 prioritizes PTSD's behavioral symptoms in four diagnostic clusters: re-experiencing, avoidance, negative cognitions and mood, and arousal. These typically cause clinically significant distress and impairment in social interactions, or other important areas of functioning.

PTSD has been subject to critiques by anthropologists since its institution into the DSM. These criticisms are largely relevant to studies in which PTSD is used to (1) construct trauma as the norm rather than the exception; (2) prioritize war-related trauma at the expense of ways in which suffering is normatively produced within the complex dynamics of political-economic regimes and ideologies; (3) privilege the individual over the social context as the locus for intervention; and (4) overemphasize negative "cultural" factors (Brewin et al. 2009). For refugees and other survivors of mass violence who endure multiple losses and stressors related to resettlement and rebuilding, trauma may not be the only difficulty they experience, but one of many producing vicious cycles that can transform transient symptoms into severe, persistent disorders (Hinton and Lewis-Fernández 2011).

Anthropologists have also inquired into the cross-cultural validity of PTSD; cross-cultural variations in trauma responses; the use of culturally available rituals, practices, and symbols; and the effectiveness of local healing responses. Hinton and Lewis-Fernández (2011) argue that several culture-bound syndromes in the DSM-IV appear co-extensive with the bio-psychological effects of PSTD. Effects include flashbacks, traumatic memories, nightmares, sleep disturbances, hypervigilance, irritability, aggression, problems with functionality and concentration, startle responses, avoidance, anxiety, depression, and panic attacks (12). Some salient culture-bound syndromes these authors mention include *susto, nervoso, pibloqtoq, latah,* windigo psychosis, *koro, khyal, ataque de nervios, haypatensi, ihahamuka, llaki,* and *masilango* (12). Hinton and Lewis-Fernández emphasize that because responses have different symptomologies, they require caution before being classified as PTSD-like syndromes. Even if DSM-defined PTSD is diagnosable in diverse cultures, it involves substantial cross-cultural variation. Some researchers see criteria, like flashbacks, as a Western cultural construction; others argue trauma responses vary so much across place and   **43** social subgroup they simply cannot be standardized (10). For others, even if PTSD does describe some universal, if abstracted, features of trauma response, local expressions of trauma-related psychopathology may be closer to people's experiences and therefore have greater clinical utility (14).

There is also a substantial literature that explores ways local practices and rituals may contribute to healing from traumatic experiences (Desjarlais 1989; Dow 1986; Frank and Frank 1991; Kirmayer 1993; Kleinman 1980; Lee, Kirmayer, and Groleau 2010; Lévi-Strauss 1963, quoted in Hinton and Kirmayer 2013, 608). These studies mitigate the individualizing tendency of the PTSD model by examining ways symptom-generation and healing are inflected with local, interpersonal, and social therapeutic mechanisms (Lester 2013b, 753). For example, mothers who lose infant children to child-hood illnesses and starvation in Northeast Brazil take some comfort by imagining their little babies growing whiter and whiter and ascending to heaven as angels (Nations 2013). This enables them to make sense of their loss and also feel the imperative to not become mired in grief. However, their suffering is hardly over. In her commentary on trauma and healing responses, Lester (2013b) gives the example of a soldier who has lost her leg. She challenges the fallacy that trauma is something that happens and then is over, rather than something that profoundly and continuously changes a person's relationship with the world. She writes, "But while that may have been the beginning and end of the specific event that caused injury to her body, it was merely the beginning of the effects of the explosion on her sense of herself, her relationships, and the world, all of which were changed in an instant and will continue to evolve over time" (755).

Hinton and Kirmayer (2013) emphasize many beneficial effects of local community attempts to recover from traumatic experiences for clinical interventions that claim cross-cultural applicability. Local healing rituals can induce positive affective states involving bodily, psychological, social, and spiritual dimensions (619). Gone's (2013) work on historical trauma promotes the value of "culture as treatment" for ways that colonization insinuates into problems of violence, drug abuse, and sexual assault among Native American peoples. He highlights the positive role that traditional rituals can play in healing intergenerational trauma and in transforming community responses to larger political injustices. Yet while violence and suffering in one generation certainly impact mental health in subsequent generations, we should not exaggerate the role of "historical trauma." This can downplay the complex historical and contemporary looping effects of structural violence, poverty, and discrimination; public discourse; and embodied experience on community adaptation and recovery (Gone 2013, 2014; Kirmayer, Gone, and Moses 2014).

44   A First-World Construct?

What about the controversial idea that trauma is a "luxury" for people living in the First World? Likewise, there are many criticisms of a diagnosis that predominantly applies to singular exceptional events (bereavement, a violent attack, sexual trauma, or natural disaster) rather than to contexts where "emergency is the rule" (Benjamin 1969). Others emphasize the tendency of the PTSD model to reduce the social, political, spiritual, and moral implications of war or genocide to strictly psychological, even biological, sets of individual consequences (Hinton and Lewis-Fernández 2011). Kleinman (1980) and Young (1995) criticize conceptions of human life as fundamentally passive and fragile and what they call the "traumatic vision" of events such as natural disasters, which for most of human history have been conceptualized as social and religious, not psychological, problems. These authors point to ways that PTSD medicalizes human suffering.

Let us examine one study that develops these arguments, Scheper-Hughes's article "A Talent for Life: Reflections on Human Vulnerability and Resistance" (2008). Drawing on fieldwork in Northeast Brazil with shantytown families, street children, and with anti-apartheid political revolutionaries in South Africa, Scheper-Hughes levels strong criticisms at the victimizing tendency of PTSD that underestimates the human capacity to survive and also thrive in extreme adversity (37). This article builds on her earlier research in Northeast Brazil on maternal reactions to infant deaths (Scheper-Hughes 1984, 1985), elaborated most fully in her book *Death Without Weeping* (1992). She argues the subjective experience of trauma can produce "paradoxical" symptoms that should be viewed as signs of resilience, not breakdown. Amidst the "invisible genocide" of extreme hunger, poverty, and high rates of infant mortality affecting this region, far from being traumatized by their children's deaths, mothers exhibit indifference, "disaffection," "detached" and emotionally empty grief responses, and even encourage their babies' deaths in morally reprehensible, possibly "insane" grief reactions: "Mother love was a fragile emotion, postponed until the newborn itself displayed a fierce will to life, a taste (gusto) and a knack (jeito) or a 'talent for life.' A high expectancy of death prepared mothers to 'let go' and even help their deselected babies to die by reducing already insufficient food, water and care" (2008: 28). They dreamt about their given up so-called angel-babies, not yet fully of the world, who had "signaled their availability for execution to their mothers who were forced into behaving like Sondercommando of the Nazi concentration camps" (28). She continues:

> The experience of too much loss, too much death where new life should be led to a kind of patient resignation (clinical psychologists would label it "accommodation syndrome") that obliterated outrage 45 as well as sorrow. No tears were wasted at an infant burial, often left in the hands of older children. Children buried children on the Alto do Cruzeiro. This practice killed two birds with one stone: it allowed mothers to absent themselves from the burial rites, and it forced children to face and accept the death of their siblings as a commonplace and unremarkable fact of life. (2008: 29)

The images she displays, such as those of children playing around infants' coffins, lend support to Scheper-Hughes's argument that "these 'resilient' survivors of childhood traumas held no grudges against their neglectful caretakers, they displayed few of the classic symptoms of trauma victims, and they viewed themselves as victors not as victims, as having met death face-to-face and won" (31)!

Maternal reactions to child deaths in this region have long concerned medical anthropologists (Lassalle and O'Dougherty 1997; Nations 2008, 2009; Rehbun 1994; Sigaud 1995). In turn, Scheper-Hughes's interpretations have generated strong controversies. As noted previously, Marilyn Nations (2013) analyzed data from the same region and period about mothers' dreams about their dead babies. She argues that mental images of infant suffering are transformed into heavenly angels in dreams precisely *so* mothers can alleviate the trauma, feelings of chronic helplessness, hopelessness, loss, and guilt they experience, and rescue themselves from the brink of clinical depression. Grieving mothers' dead-baby dreams alleviate infant death trauma, crippling self-blame, and preserve their own mental sanity, illustrated in the following quote: "You see, the only thing a poor woman truly owns that no one can borrow, cheat, steal or rob from her ... is her imagination!' (Dona Chiquinha grieving the death of her 10 children, Pacatuba, Ceará, Brazil)" (632). Nations goes on to accuse Scheper-Hughes of gross inaccuracy, moral recklessness, and "interpretive violence" (678) for downplaying the acute trauma and complicated grief mothers *do* suffer over the deaths of their children. Instead she argues that interpretations of mourning should be contextualized within local moral worlds to avoid demoralizing grieving Brazilian mothers and compounding their suffering.

In short, anthropologists have provided important critiques concerning PTSD's cross-cultural applicability and have raised serious ethical questions. These questions concern texts that may reinforce pathologized representations of communities that are already suffering from chronic oppression and structural violence.

Trauma as Politics

As a psychiatric category, PTSD is one of the few disorders defined by its causes, not exclusively its behavioral symptomology. PTSD overwhelmingly involves military populations, displacees, refugees, and asylum seekers who are victims of war and humanitarian interventions or must present themselves as such to access aid or forms of physical and economic mobility inaccessible otherwise. Anthropologists have revealed how the categories of "migrant" and "asylum seeker" are related to the ways medical knowledge shapes diverse encounters with power (Farmer 2005; Fassin and Rechtman 2009; Kleinman and Kleinman 1991). They have highlighted how the legal and bureaucratic regulation of the suffering of asylum seekers prioritizes factual and political categories over an experiential understanding of a person's world (Das 2007b: 330), and how racialized ideas of anachronism and cultural primitivism about the immigrant Other play out in discourses and diagnoses of trauma (Khan 2013b).

Allan Young's monograph *The Harmony of Illusions* (1995) is a seminal text in the development of the anthropology of psychiatry and work on trauma and PTSD, particularly in relation to war. Young queries the assumption of a link between the memories of traumatic events and an individual's symptoms. Given psychiatry has dispatched "causes" from most disorders, PTSD is unique. Young shows how diagnoses force the flow of time into a directional arc that begins with a cause and ends with traumatic memory and PTSD symptoms. Reinterpreting earlier anthropological work on shell-shock, Young presents another possibility: disturbing symptoms cause disturbing memories, not the reverse. Evolving out of conceptions of human nature, and psychiatry's development since the 1870s as a clinical specialism, he views PTSD as being inseparable from the diagnostic technologies, moral divisions and economies, and legal decision making that determine responses to military populations. Young also uses ethnographic insights and transcripts of therapy in a psychiatric unit treating Vietnam War veterans. Here, patients' narratives, institutional imperatives, and therapeutic models all coalesce in ways PTSD diagnoses filter into veterans' disordered realities.

PTSD is therefore unusual insofar as it operates as a diagnosis and a political metaphor. It is produced by clinical psychiatry but also by international politics. Its symptomology bears crucially on questions of legal expertise and responsibility, compensation, culpability, and human rights. For example, ideas of a traumatized populace were incorporated into justifications for "regime change" (i.e., invasion and occupation) in Afghanistan (Abu-Lughod 2002). In Haiti, Erica Caple James's (2010) ethnography of military and humanitarian intervention explores how not everybody's trauma is viewed equally. Following the violent events surrounding the coup in 1991, she reveals the hierarchies that were created in ways the traumas of some victims were denied by US officials, and only recognized selectively by other humanitarian providers. Drawing on accounts of women survivors, she shows how the corruption and competition among individuals working in development and humanitarian organizations led political and psychosocial initiatives to ultimately fail. 47

Historically, the dominant trauma model PTSD derives from is an intellectual genealogy dating back to Hobbes and Locke, through Freud and psychoanalysis. PTSD originated in studies of veterans of the two World Wars who were suffering from what was variously termed shell-shock, combat stress, battle fatigue, and war neurosis. The DSM-III diagnosis of post-traumatic stress disorder provided a more sympathetic response to US veterans who had been involved in appalling barbarity in wars in Korea and Vietnam. Young (2002) examines the notion of the "self-traumatized perpetrator." He argues PTSD is a "transient mental illness" that is closely dependent on the political and social issues of war surrounding its emergence and predicted it was likely to vanish with them. Yet far from disappearing, the DSM-III diagnosis expanded exponentially to include peacetime traumas such as natural disasters, terrorist attacks, domestic violence, rape, incest, occupational hazards, and experiences of cancer. This was also due to efforts by feminist psychiatrists to recognize the severity of sexual and domestic violence (Herman 1992), and by military psychiatrists to recognize the injured soldier as deserving compensation and support.

Trauma's expansion foreshadowed what Fassin and Rechtman analyze as a major reshaping of our moral economy in their book *The Empire of Trauma* (2009) (for reviews see Anderson 2010; Das 2010; Kraus 2010). This book examines how "trauma has become a major signifier of our age" in explanations of a "plurality of ills," including rape, genocide, torture, slavery, terrorist attacks, and natural disasters (xi). The authors draw on fieldwork in France among organizations providing psychiatric aid to victims of a chemical explosion, organizations in the Palestinian territories, and organizations defending asylum seekers. They show how trauma has become viewed as both a cause of suffering and a resource that may be used to support a right or mobilize mental health professionals in new fields related to humanitarian psychiatry. Let us examine these claims in more detail.

First, Fassin and Rechtman (2009) historicize how, as a "new language of the event," suspicion about trauma gave way to the value of proof

(6–7). Part One explores trauma's conceptual growth from the 1860s when applied to victims of railway accidents, to psychoanalysts' ideas of trauma neurosis and the repression of painful memories. While during World War I "trauma insanity" threatened the glorified ideal of heroic soldiers, survivors of Nazi concentration camps in World War II were clearly not malingerers. Subsequently, "survivor syndrome" emerged and transformed traumatic experience into a "testament to the unspeakable" (72) and survivors into victims "broken by what they had witnessed and by what they had done" (91). Part Two, "The Politics of Reparation," illustrates the rise of psychiatric victimology in the 1990s when victims' rights organizations began campaigning using notions of psychic trauma. Now, "it was victims who justified victimology, not the reverse" (126). Discourse also began to differentiate victims between the "most exposed," "the most vulnerable" individuals or "the most disadvantaged" social groups (143), and as a result they benefited differentially from compensation payouts and recognition.

Part Three covers the rise of humanitarian psychiatry, presenting examples from wars in Armenia, Bosnia, Kosovo, and Palestine (Fassin and Rechtman 2009: 158). The new field of humanitarian psychiatry "manifests as a stirring of empathy rather than a call for clinical evaluation" (177). In Palestine, humanitarian psychiatrists have joined journalists, lawyers, politicians, and religious leaders in bearing witness to psychological distress and denouncing human rights violations (216). Part Four addresses clinical practices of asylum, torture and the notion of evidence on the body, and activist doctors (255). The authors show how the refugee mind and body, classified and diagnosed as suffering from trauma, become literally "incorporated" as tools governing a humanitarian gateway to European citizenship. They locate the body seeking asylum as a site of political power and truth, and show how the authority of medical certificates in citizenship cases erases the personal experience of asylum seekers as political subjects. French medics write reports that emphasize the victims' psychic scars, but this prevents them from adequately treating their patients. The book concludes with a grand statement: "The validity people are willing to accord to trauma in order to relate the experience of descendants of survivors of the Holocaust, of Armenian or Rwandan genocide, of victims of slavery or apartheid, is not the validity of a clinical category but rather of a judgement—the judgment of history" (284).

Beyond Trauma?

This final section points to just some ways anthropologists have sought alternatives to the dominance of trauma as the explanatory framework for the consequences of critical events. First, let us return to Freud's original thesis. In *Beyond the Pleasure Principle*, Freud ([1920] 2003) theorized the psychic compulsion to repeat traumatic events as deriving from a tendency toward self-destruction and an attempt to accept the reality of death. His theory emphasizes a formulation of history as an endless repetition of previous violence. It has received innumerable critiques, mostly in literary theory, but also in the humanities and in anthropology.

Das (2007a) critiques the tendency of social scientists to interpret violence through trauma. She argues that individual and collective trauma are too often elided and also linked to compulsive-repetitive interpretations that "short-circuit the complex ways in which we might understand how particular regions of the past are actualized" (103). She argues for the need to develop more subtle relations of violence, time, and language. More precisely, she proposes that an analytical "descent into the ordinary" (7) can reveal how the violence of critical events becomes expressed in ways of relatedness in everyday life, for example in "how feelings of skepticism come to be embedded within a frayed everyday life so that guarantees of belonging to larger entities such as communities or state are not capable of erasing the hurts or providing means of repairing this sense of being betrayed by the everyday" (9).

Next, anthropologists have challenged studies that uncritically prioritize the traumatic consequences of war-related violence and loss, and support understandings of the magnitude of war-related PTSD, psychiatric disorders, and adjustment challenges in countries of origin and abroad (Miller and Rasmussen 2010). They recognize that adjustment undeniably stresses the mental health of refugees. However, they also stress that explanations centered exclusively on trauma shift attention away from the less visible conditions in local and global economies that affect the ability of migrants and citizens to work.

Hollan (2013) argues that work may promote a positive self-image that can redress the humiliation and vulnerability associated with experiences of trauma. Notably, reintegration or realignment with social norms is not always evidence that recovery has occurred. People's processes of "retethering" to the world may include behaviors that are pathological in psychiatric terms (Lester 2013b: 754). Likewise, "normal" labor conditions may themselves be exploitative, oppressive, or traumatic. As Harvey (2000) observes, under contemporary capitalism, "sickness" is the inability to work. He points to work itself as the source of traumatic suffering. While global inequalities and rapid technological change have produced "spaces of hope" across the globe, dreams of "making it" are often lost in the soulless reality of migrant life, and in the traumatic "romanticism of endlessly open projects" that never close (174).

Hope is therefore interesting because it describes a state of fantasy, unreality, or sometimes totally unrealizable condition of clinging to and coping with the impossible. In a Freudian economy of traumatic suffering, hope circumvents grief. It is a stubborn means of denying reality and fear of change that effectively paralyzes other functions, preserves the link with what one has lost, and "guarantees lack of change, lack of mourning and the least expenditure of energy" (Potamianou 1997: 3–4).

I have studied meanings of *khapgan* (Pashto, feeling down) among Afghan migrants in the UK (Khan 2013a). In Pashto, *khapgan* generally connotes depression, and also frustration, and it may be expressed aggressively in self-recrimination, blame, or punishment. *Khapgan* is intense, protracted, and links to trauma-like feelings of *dar* (fear, panic); *warkhata* (lost door), meaning shock, sudden loss of confidence; *khata* (endangered); *badyaad* (bad memories); *khapa wacht* (sad times); *khapakai*, meaning to feel strangled, as if one is drowning or being choked; or simply *ze naroghyum* (I feel ill) (521). *Khapgan* points to psychiatric symptoms but also to the salience of hope in ways migrants assume, challenge, and reshape their load of cultural control and economic obligations. Again, drawing from a single case study, I argue that the inability to move or work may enfold attempts (but I stress, not as a choice) to repace or even stop oppressive realities conceived in terms of "too much movement" or too much hope.

Let us end with one powerful attempt to stretch the language of trauma. Drawing on the languages of psychoanalysis and also neuroscience, Malabou (2012) poses a confrontation between Freudian and neurological approaches to traumatic wounding. She develops the concept of "destructive plasticity" to describe the loss of emotion in people she calls the "new wounded." These may be victims of neurological lesions or attacks, degenerative brain diseases, Alzheimer's disease, schizophrenia, autistism, and epilepsy, or indeed anybody who has been radically severed from their past by brain damage (10). Malabou identifies some problems in Freudian psychoanalysis for interpreting the experience of victims of cerebral trauma. For these "new wounded," she argues that the "post" in "post-traumatic stress disorder" is simply not relevant. Psychoanalysis has no language to speak about those "lost persons" of neurotrauma who do not "regress," or repeat the past, but instead "shatter" because their histories are simply erased (84). These people are not traumatized, in Freudian terms, but disaffected after physical trauma has annihilated their identity (49).

In conclusion, this chapter has highlighted just some of the manifold directions that research in anthropology has taken around the concept and classification of trauma. These understandings highlight personal and collective meanings associated with past events, and patterns of coping with loss and violence. Many local interpretations of suffering also correspond with psychiatric criteria for PTSD. This focus may interest clinicians wishing to develop understandings of trauma responses in migration contexts and increasing forms of precariousness in "Western" societies, as psychiatric criteria themselves become increasingly subject to global migration. The criticism that PTSD pathologizes normal distress also raises difficult questions around how much impairment can be tolerated before it is reasonable to regard symptoms as abnormal. Last, PTSD is uniquely shaped by psychiatry's interactions with political and legal institutions. These interactions establish what qualifies as diagnostic criteria, evidence, and an appropriate outcome following treatments. Ongoing investigations emphasize ways that understandings of PTSD prioritize a coalition of historical contingencies, legal evidence, and international politics alongside psychiatric research.

Discussion and Activities

Trauma is a culture-bound syndrome that applies most aptly in contexts where trauma is the exception, not the norm. Discuss.

Given "trauma" is used to market hair and skin products, as well as describe the symptoms following violent assaults, war experiences, and so on, has the concept become so generalized in everyday discourse as to become meaningless? Have we all experienced trauma in some form?

How has the intellectual history of the concept of trauma traveled from religious meanings to psychoanalysis and psychiatrization in the DSM, and from the politics of humanitarianism to human rights and military intervention?

Examine online stories of asylum seekers or refugees. What "political languages" shape the telling of individual experiences? How do they compare with the scientific, "reductionist" writing styles on asylum seeker medical certificates? For whom are these stories of interest, and why are they necessary?

Review a selection of online sites of homeless veterans' programs (e.g., Veterans Village, Wounded Warriors), and examine the message, construction, and ethics and politics of the representation of war, patriotism, and nationalism expressed through the language of trauma. This should address the discursive and political relationship between the military, the public, the serving soldier, and the homeless veteran.

Conduct a critical analysis of a collective account of traumatic suffering. Examples can include representations, testimonies, and witness accounts from the Holocaust, the Cambodian Genocide Trials, the South African Truth and Reconciliation Commission, riots, conflicts, or situations of forced displacement and exile. Assess the ways in which collective and individual accounts both correspond and differ.

Additional Films and Readings

Films

40 Years of Silence: An Indonesian Tragedy. 2009. Directed by Robert Lemelson. Los Angeles: Elemental Productions.

Poster Girl. 2010. Directed by Sara Nesson. Mitchell Block.

Readings

Abramovitz, Sharon, and Catherine Panter-Brick, eds. 2015. *Medical Humanitarianism and Ethnographies of Practice*. Philadelphia: University of Pennsylvania Press.

Davis, Kelly Ray. 2015. *Addicted. Pregnant. Poor*. Durham, NC: Duke University Press.

Fassin, Didier, and Estelle D'Halluin. 2005. "The Truth from the Body: Medical Certificates as Ultimate Evidence for Asylum Seekers." *American Anthropologist* 107: 597–608.

Finlay, Erin. 2015. "The Few, the Proud: Women Combat Veterans and Post-Traumatic Stress Disorder in the United States." In *Global Mental Health: Anthropological Perspectives*, edited by Brandon Kohrt and Emily Mendenhall, 221–38. Walnut Creek, CA: Left Coast Press.

James, Erica C. 2010. *Democratic Insecurities: Violence, Trauma, and Intervention in Haiti*. Berkeley: University of California Press.

Mattingly, Cheryl. 2010. *The Paradox of Hope. Journeys through a Clinical Borderland*. Berkeley: University of California Press.

Rousseau, Cécile, and Laurence Kirmayer. 2009. "Cultural Adaptation of Psychological Trauma Treatment for Children 'Letter to Editor.'" *Journal of the American Academy of Child and Adolescent Psychiatry 48*: 954–55.

Shaarawi, Nadia. 2015. "Life in Transit: Mental Health, Temporality, and Urban Displacement for Iraqi Refugees." In *Global Mental Health: Anthropological Perspectives*, edited by Brandon Kohrt and Emily Mendenhall, 73–86. Walnut Creek, CA: Left Coast Press.

Snodgrass, Jeffrey. 2015. "Festive Fighting and Forgiving: Ritual and Resilience among Indigenous Indian 'Conservation Refugees.'" In *Global Mental Health: Anthropological Perspectives*, edited by Brandon Kohrt and Emily Mendenhall, 173–90. Walnut Creek, CA: Left Coast Press.

CHAPTER 5

"THE BIG THREE": SCHIZOPHRENIA, DEPRESSION, AND BIPOLAR DISORDER

"At first I feel calm then 'boom,' suddenly the illness comes. I get a dry cough and suddenly I can't breathe. The spirits drop by and they look for me. When I'm sound asleep, they look for me. They look for my memory."

"There are sounds coming from the grass. I see these black things, these apparitions. While I cut the grass they wander around. When I look I see they are also in the middle of the rice field. It was like that. There were lots of voices ... When I wander in the fields, they're always there. ... Usually they try to enter into our body. ... They say take care of us. Prepare offerings for us. I do less work in the fields. ... My enthusiasm wanes. I just want to hide. I just want to find an empty and quiet place."

These quotations are taken from Lemelson's compelling film *Shadows and Illuminations* (2010b). It is based on fieldwork in rural Bali, which took place more than one century after Kraepelin's ([1904] 2000) early venture into cross-cultural psychiatry in Java. Lemelson tells the story of Pak Kereta, a man afflicted with voices, revealing multiple explanations of how Kereta understands his illness. These include the grief he and his wife experienced after losing their second child; pesticide poisoning from eating contaminated eels; terror during the anticommunist killings in Indonesia in 1965 when over one million people died and Kereta, a Communist, witnessed killings, including that of his father (it is unclear if Kereta killed people); visits by spirits in Bali's Hindu, Buddhist, and animist traditions who punish him for sins in a previous life; witchcraft (*ngeb*); and "paranoid schizophrenia," the diagnosis given him by a local psychiatrist. Kereta seeks help from traditional healers who are by turns ineffective and harmful, anti-psychotic medicines, and his wife's support and forbearance. Lemelson shows how

Kereta's experience of his condition is shaped by the particular avenues of help available to him. His personal strategy for protection is to wear his army jacket and helmet. These protect Kereta from his spirits and allow him to sleep, work in the rice fields, and find peace. This poignant film demonstrates how vastly different classificatory and treatment systems can coexist. Lemelson shows that it is precisely the lack of a definitive label that allows Kereta to explore different ways of living with his spirits and voices.

This chapter addresses the "big three" most commonly diagnosed psychiatric disorders: schizophrenia, bipolar disorder, and depression. Although schizophrenia and bipolar disorder have different underlying causes (psychosis, neurosis), their symptomologies overlap, especially in terms of depression. All three have been subject to debates regarding the primacy of biological, cultural, or social "causes"; variations in cultural understandings; and assumptions of poor prognosis. The "big three" nexus provides a rich ground for analyzing religious institutions and spirit possession, different forms of psychiatry, and mental health activism. This chapter first examines the history of the big three disorders in psychiatry. Next, it explores some key studies associated with the "big three" topic. This raises several interesting questions. In what ways do local religious ideas and cultural imagery influence interpretations of severe mental illness? To what extent can meaningful social roles and support networks promote positive outcomes for people with severe mental health problems? In what ways is "high-functioning" mental illness "rewarded" in contemporary society? And how do our own systems of mental health care promote or foreclose opportunities for therapeutic communities and social models of care?

Historical Developments

Mental illness in psychiatry and psychoanalysis historically comprised two main categories: "melancholia" and "mania." These are the two oldest known mental disorders. Melancholia bears on the modern diagnosis depression, whereas "mania" relates to schizophrenia and bipolar disorder. Descriptions of melancholia appear in Ancient Greek and Egyptian writings, and in Burton's *Anatomy of Melancholy* ([1621] 2001). However, modern definitions of mania and depression largely originate in definitions of *dementia praecox* (precocious madness), particularly that of Emil Kraepelin ([1893] 1990). In Kraepelin's conceptualization, *dementia praecox* was a biological brain disease that resulted in "irreversible deterioration." Kraepelin divided nineteenth-century psychiatric taxonomies into two classes: manic depressive psychosis (ameliorable) and *dementia praecox* (incurable, degenerate). The Kraepelinian dichotomy impacted twentieth-century psychiatry, especially the bifurcation of Axis 1 and Axis 2 type disorders (Luhrmann 2001). Axis 1 includes schizophrenia, major depression, bipolar disorder, PTSD, and dissociative and obsessive-compulsive disorders (46). Axis 2 refers to neurotic disorders originating in psychoanalytic traditions, including personality and mood disorders such as borderline, narcissistic, bipolar (without psychosis) schizoid, and antisocial (47). By contrast, classical psychoanalysis recognized three exclusive mental structures: neurosis, psychosis, and perversion. The psychoses contained another three structures—paranoia, schizophrenia, and melancholia (Leader 2011: 74). These early definitions were frequently misinterpreted and subject to change. Importantly, there is still no conclusive explanation of the causes of the "big three" mental disorders. But let us briefly examine some definitions below.

Etymologically, schizophrenia means "splitting" or "shattering" the mind. Eugen Bleuler ([1911] 1950) originally theorized the term in 1908; Pinel recorded the earliest case in France in 1809. Bleuler described four main symptoms: flattened affect, autism, impaired association of ideas, and ambivalence (the "four As") (Stotz-Ingenlath 2000). In his book, *The Psychopathic Personalities* (1958), Schneider emphasized biological causes and later added 12 "first rank symptoms" to his classification (1959). These included delusions of being controlled by an external force; thought insertion, thought withdrawal, and thought broadcasting; and hearing voices that discuss one's behavior or converse with other voices. Schneider (1959) proposed that diagnoses of psychosis should analyze the meaning of a delusional idea in the person's life over its content. Notwithstanding, the subsequent emphasis on behavioral symptoms in psychiatry effectively removed the "problem" of analyzing meaning from psychosis.

The modern concept of bipolar disorder originates in definitions of "tension insanity" (Kahlbaum 1874), "manic stupor," and "manic-depressive insanity" (Kraepelin [1893] 1990). In the 1840s, French psychiatrists Falret and Baillarger conceptualized "circular madness" and "double form madness" to distinguish "madness" from mania and depression in other disorders. However, Kraepelin classified them together under the inclusive category "manic-depressive insanity," and his ideas dominated. After the mid-twentieth century, studies again differentiated bipolar from unipolar depression (Angst 1966; Leonhard 1957; Perris 1966). "Classic" bipolar disorder came to characterize a mixed state comprising mania, euphoria, grandiosity, flight of ideas, pressurized speech, hypersexuality, depression, anxiety, irritability, sleep disturbances, suicidal ideation, gross motor retardation, and psychosis.

Depression has been theorized as melancholia, neurasthenia, clinical depression, depression, a major depressive disorder, a malady of the elite (of writers, artists, and great thinkers including Plato and Socrates), a biochemical problem of neurotransmitters, an imbalance in the body's four humors, a sin, and a construct of pharmaceutical interests (Lawlor 2012). Kraepelin first referred to melancholia in terms of depressive states. Schneider (1920) subsequently differentiated *endogenous depression*, biological in origin, from *reactive depression,* referring to a trait or situational response. Freud ([1917] 2005, [1920] 2003) contributed arguments about grief and loss in regard to "healthy" mourning and the more "perverse" form melancholia.

How are these disorders organized in the DSM-5? First, the DSM-5 clusters together many specified and unspecified schizophrenia spectrum and psychotic disorders. Schizophrenia is diagnosed by the presence of delusions, hallucinations, disorganized speech, grossly disorganized or catatonic behavior, negative symptoms, and impaired social functioning. Bipolar-type schizoaffective disorder represents a kind of hybrid. Differentiating between schizoaffective disorder, bipolar disorder, and acute polymorphic disorders can challenge psychiatrists. Second, the DSM-5 bipolar spectrum disorders expand on Kraepelin's (1893) four classifications of mania: hypomania; acute mania, delusional, or psychotic mania; mixed states; and depressive or anxious mania. The main types are bipolar 1 ("classic" bipolar); bipolar 2 (involving hypomanic episodes, but not full-blown mania); cyclothymic disorder; mixed states; and rapid cycling. Whereas the ICD-10 requires two discrete mood episodes, the DSM-5 diagnosis requires just one lifetime manic episode. Bipolar disorder often co-occurs with PTSD, panic, anxiety, substance misuse, and major depressive disorders. Third, the cluster "Depressive Disorders" includes disruptive mood dysregulation disorder, major depressive disorder, persistent depressive disorder, premenstrual disorder, medication-induced depressive disorder, and other variations. Symptoms include fatigue, insomnia, psychomotor agitation or retardation, feelings of worthlessness, inappropriate guilt, impaired cognition and social functioning, indecisiveness, and suicidal ideation. Melancholia is specified as a depression subtype.

Depression

In this section we look at how anthropologists have approached the "big three" disorders of schizophrenia, bipolar disorder, and depression. Discussions about depression in anthropology have revolved around a major clinical disorder, a cultural idiomatic expression of everyday distress, and a normative-pathological response to modern labor conditions. Regarding the diagnosis of "depression" in Buddhist Sri Lanka, Obeyesekere (1985) asks, Do members of a culture need to collectively understand the category "depression" in order to "really" be depressed (1985)? Is depression "there," regardless of what the individual thinks? Where do we locate meaning if nobody in the culture accepts the diagnosis? How far can we speak of cultural "equivalences"? He questions how the diagnosis of depression in Sri Lanka might apply when sorrow is not viewed as an *illness* but as intrinsic to larger cultural, philosophical, and local cosmologies that emphasize the importance of suffering in understanding problems of existence. He criticizes the idea that depression is "universal with culture-bound varia-tions" (137). Instead, he emphasizes the ways depression becomes culturally positive and meaningful: "The *work of culture* is the process whereby painful motives and affects such as those occurring in depression are transformed into publicly accepted sets of meanings and symbols" (147; emphasis in original). In developing these questions, Obeyesekere cites Brown and Harris's 1978 study of poor British women who, according to clinicians, are depressed even though they do not know it. He also refers to Ashanti and Yoruba individuals who perversely "refuse" to conform to Western psychi-atric norms of depression. Instead, they interpret their experiences as part of an existential condition related to the "natural vicissitudes of life" (135).

Kleinman (1986) elaborated some similar themes regarding cultural translation in his classic study in China. He observed that many Chinese hospital patients met the American criteria for major depression. However, they conceived of their problems as neurasthenia (headaches, fatigue, dizzi-ness, insomnia, anxiety, etc.). This posed a "problem" because neurasthenia, which describes a physical, nervous condition rather than an emotional one, had become defunct in American psychiatry. Furthermore, neurasthenia afflicted many people whose lives were destroyed during the Cultural Revolution. Despite treatment, these patients did not improve. Kleinman argued these should not be seen as cases of individual "disease" but as part of a cultural history, and they should be recognized as "illness experiences" of social suffering. Responding to Kleinman, Shweder (1988) criticizes the DSM's symptoms list as a blunt instrument for representing major suffering. He asks, *Can* Kleinman's Chinese patients diagnosed with neurasthenia *also* be diagnosed, using the DSM, with depression (482)? Are neurasthenia and depression different labels for the same suffering, or are they different kinds of suffering? Neurasthenia and depression *may* co-occur, as they do in Kleinman's study, but they will not always. Therefore, using the DSM may lead to the false classification of neurasthenia as depression, or the false conclusion that neurasthenia *is* depression (484). These questions about cultural and conceptual equivalence concern what typically describes the "category fallacy" (Kleinman 1977).

Several analysts have linked forms of depression to the stresses of modern life. Importantly, this does not mean depression is a "choice." People do not "choose" severe mental pain, for example, to avoid work-ing. Kitanaka (2011) studies how the "rise" of depression in Japan is linked to conditions of work. She traces the historical progress of conceptual debates through the twentieth century about neurasthenia as a disorder of overwork or "weak" personality, through to Western ideas of melancholia (a melancholic "type") linked to physical and mental stagnation. She makes links between the proliferation of depression in Japan as a new "national disease" (2) and the unrewarded Japanese man who has overinternalized the tradition of hard work, corporate loyalty, and productivity (9). She shows how depression becomes interpreted by physicians and sufferers as a disease of fatigue and work stress (61) that is treated by pharmaceuticals rather than by social structures that determine overwork. In Japan, biological causes are not politically controversial as they are in the US, where they are linked to racism, especially around poor and minoritized communities. Rather, in Japan they are used successfully by psychiatrists to persuade patients that they are suffering from a biological pathology. In turn, this makes depression a socially legitimate disease. In tracking how depression becomes recognized, pathologized, and drugged, Kitanaka raises a complicated problem concerning the emergence (or "colonization") of a mental illness that alleviates suffering for many people but also aggravates distress and uncertainty for many others. Yet the rise of depression in Japan is not all positive. For example, suicide loses its traditional positive, moral meanings. Last, the inevitable limitations of antidepressants as a "cure-all" serve paradoxically to produce chronically depressed "intractable" patients—at the same time as they cast doubts on psychiatry's idealistic therapeutic promise (185).

The Manic Market

There are fewer ethnographic studies of bipolar disorder than of schizophrenia and depression. This may be because the huge resurgence in diagnoses of bipolar disorder has occurred relatively recently. Leader (2013: 1) cynically observes that since the mid-1990s, when new drugs (anti-psychotics, mood stabilizers, and antidepressants) emerged that could target subtler "bipolar" mood changes, diagnoses among Americans increased 4,000 per cent.

One important study is Emily Martin's book *Bipolar Expeditions* (2007), which links the manic-depressive patterns of bipolar disorder to forms of (dys)function in modern American economic culture. Martin draws on fieldwork with manic-depressive support groups, psychiatrists, examples from popular culture, and her personal experience of living with the diagnosis of bipolar disorder. She examines how the binary concepts of rationality and irrationality shape understandings of mania, which has long been associated in Western thinking with madness—and reflects on the extent to which she herself is a "rational" person. She highlights the contradiction in the way mania is attributed with ideas of insanity, while its characteristic energy and creativity are admired and associated with "rational" economic success.

Martin (2007) describes some problematic formations from late modernity in the current psychiatric criteria of bipolar disorder in the individual who is considered either "*too* energized, or *too* immobilized" (46). She revisits Kraepelin's 1893 definition of manic-depressive insanity, which emerged after the Industrial Revolution amidst anxieties concerning "simple exposure to the hectic pace and excessive stimuli of modern life," and co-occurred with symptoms of a depressive, fragmented, alienated consciousness and isolation from the social (52). In the contemporary United States where the economic dominates the social, cultural forces are pushing all social relations to be mediated through the market: "Experiences of mania, once considered a sign of fearful and disordered irrationality, have come to epitomize the vital energy—found in the psyche rather than the laboring body—that the market *needs* to keep expanding. This is the heart of the affinity between contemporary American culture and the characteristics of manic depression" (54). In Martin's argument, the forces of modernity and late capitalism do not "cause" mental illness, but they provide a forceful, deadly site for it to flourish:

> In the world of financial markets, commentators on the economy often speak of alternation between extreme highs and lows as a disease, and sometimes describe it as a form of "manic depression." But in practice, for the adept, such volatility can act as a resource, because the volatility provides profit-taking possibilities for those who can anticipate when the market will shift either way. Mania's interstitial position between mood (floating, changeable feelings in the psyche) and motivation (organized, goal-directed behavior) is crucial for understanding why the "manic" artist or CEO seems to function well in the corporate world of the twenty-first century, but the "manic market" is a harbinger of disaster. (234)

Let us examine her book in more detail. In Part One, "Manic Depression as Experience," Martin (2007) discusses the concepts of movement and control. Drawing on fieldwork with bipolar support groups, she highlights some tensions in the way people with bipolar disorder experience mania as something they have power over and can control, and also as something that controls or possesses them. These tensions around control and lack of control, and mania and depression, divide people's worlds into multiple experiences of "different" personalities and types of self. Rather than occurring as "either-or" extremes, Martin argues that people's experiences of mania and depression are multiple, sometimes concurrent, states on a continuum that invoke anxieties around their ability to control their movement along it. In bipolar support meetings, scientific classifications play a key part in social performance. Rather than reject the language of psychiatry for more emotional or personal kinds of self-expression, Martin found to her surprise that people used scientific language to legitimate their experience, exert control, and protect themselves from too much scrutiny (80).

Part Two, "Mania as a Resource," explores mania as a metaphor and a myth driving the financial and business markets and popular cultural television shows, films, and art (Martin 2007: 202). Martin (2007) presents us images of financial traders and stockbrokers who work without sleep, entrepreneurs involved simultaneously in multiple high-risk ventures, and corporate training programs that "teach" people to be manic to maximize their success and productivity. She takes the example of the comedian Robin Williams who had a diagnosis of bipolar disorder. While his high-octane performances give an appearance of being in control, his speech is characterized by loose associations, distractibility, and high levels of manic energy. Framing manic behavior as an economic resource allows fluctuations in the stock market to be interpreted as symptoms of the market's bipolar disorder, where the aim is to not let "animal spirits" control rational thinking (276). In a similar pattern, sufferers of bipolar disorder are encouraged to chart (and appear to control) their moods on mood charts like stock prices.

Martin (2007) uses bipolar disorder as a metaphor for explaining some dimensions of rationality, irrationality, mood, and motivation pervading American economic and cultural life. Given that the US and global financial markets collapsed one year after the book's publication, and Robin Williams committed suicide in 2014, her arguments about the precariousness of individual and societal control over mania are remarkably prescient.

Schizophrenia, Social Recovery, Sacrifice

Previous chapters examined some anthropological research on schizophrenia that implicates shamanism and ritual healing, variations in local and psychiatric interpretations, and ways social support and public attitudes influence people's experiences of their condition. Certainly the social context and meanings of auditory hallucinations (hearing voices) may influence the prognosis for schizophrenia. Comparing the content of auditory hallucinations across three countries, Luhrmann, Padmavati, Tharoor, and Osei (2015) found that US patients understand that hearing voices denotes "craziness" and often conceal their experiences of intrusive and unreal thoughts. In Ghana, local explanations include being under "spiritual attack" by spirits or witches, but voices are also viewed as morally good and powerful. This explanation carries less stigma than schizophrenia and can involve many positive experiences. These authors propose these differences can be explained by "social kindling": people with serious psychotic disorders interpret auditory events via "cultural invitations" or variations in ways of thinking about minds, persons, and spirits. Analyzing local relationships to auditory hallucinations has the potential to improve prognoses for a diagnosis dominated by ideas of "neural deficit."

Regarding social factors, Japan has some of the world's highest institutionalization rates for people with schizophrenia. In her ethnography *A Disability of the Soul: An Ethnography of Schizophrenia and Mental Illness in*

Japan, Nakamura (2013) locates these within Japan's post–twentieth-century history of mass institutionalization, eugenic sterilization, antipsychotic "revolution," and pressures from families to sequester sick relatives. In her book, and the DVD-film accompanying the book titled *Bethel*, Nakamura focuses on a self-supporting, Christian-based therapeutic community for members with schizophrenia in northern Japan and gives us a touching portrait of the lives of Bethel's members. She emphasizes the central role of the social values of work and community support, and she critiques the idea of a "cure." Instead, she demonstrates the central importance of "becoming a social being." Bethel's members achieve this through participating in social therapies, work, and events such as the Hallucinations and Delusions Grand Prix. Institutional and social support is crucial for stability and for living full and productive lives. The Bethel therapeutic community eschews a clinical approach for a more social approach to dealing with mental health problems. This community is all about fostering relationships, but not necessarily individual relationships; rather, they encourage members to come to terms with themselves as social beings.

61

This collective approach aims to help people live with mental illness rather than attempt to cure or eradicate their symptoms. The Bethel film shows that less stigmatizing labels, flexible work routines, meaningful social roles, and networks of support are effective in promoting ongoing well-being and positive outcomes for people with schizophrenia. It provides an interesting counterpoint to Corin and Lauzon's (1992) findings, for example, that in the US, schizophrenics fared better when they practiced positive social withdrawal *outside* institutions. This contrast between the United States and Japan begs some reflection on how broad ideologies of societal individualism or collectivism bear on the formation and effectiveness of particular treatment regimes.

The task of capturing advances in biological psychiatry alongside an appreciation of cultural difference is not easy, but it is essential. Jenkins and Barratt's collection *Schizophrenia, Culture and Subjectivity* (2004) features case studies from Bangladesh, Borneo, Indonesia, Africa, and North and South America. Following a preface by Arthur Kleinman, the book examines schizophrenia as a paradigm for understanding "fundamental human processes and capacities for experience" (29). It explores connections between the ordinary, extraordinary, subjective, intersubjective, and social, and illuminates ethnographic ideas such as "stress," "recovery," and the "symptoms of colonialism" within broader framings of culture, self, and experience; experiences of schizophrenia; and subjectivity and emotion. In the collection, Good and Subandi examine the case of an Indonesian woman, Yani, whose psychotic experiences may or may not fit the DSM-IV criteria for schizophrenia. They develop a Javanese context of interpretation that emphasizes the interplay between the axes of power/impotency, danger/protection, and physical/occult factors to highlight a shared cultural repertoire of interpretations between cosmopolitan professionals and poor urban residents. In her chapter, Corin queries how realities become reconstituted after a psychotic break, and she analyzes silence and withdrawal as "embodied banks in an oversignifying reality as an attempt to stop the drift of significance" (139). While James Wilce employs a microlinguistic analysis, Sue Estroff analyzes the politics of personal narrative. This important book is prescient in arguing that culturally informed local analyses are essential for confronting the social and political conditions of global health care and for decentering Western epistemological assumptions and ontological interpretations of extreme experiences in non-Western settings—but the rise of pharmaceuticals and biopsychiatry is rendering them less viable or likely to be consulted by practitioners.

Our last study in this chapter is Scheper-Hughes's book *Saints, Scholars, and Schizophrenics* (2001). Scheper-Hughes examines the high rates of suicide and mental illness in a small farming community she calls "Ballybran." This book analyzes what Scheper-Hughes describes as the pathogenic stresses that contribute to high rates of psychological tragedy, schizophrenia, deep clinical depressions, and adult suicide among farmers in rural Ireland in the 1970s. Similar to her interpretations of mothers' responses to infant deaths in Northeast Brazil (1992, 2008), here she reveals another "extraordinary drama of masked violence and sacrifice" (42). In these families, parents need to retain one son to care for the farm and for them in their dotage, and they sacrifice their sons: "For the potential farm heirs of today are prepared from early childhood for their destined role by a subtle but persistent process of victimization and scapegoating on the part of parents, siblings and the community at large. It is this ego-deflating process, I hypothesize, that contributes to the high rate of psychosis (especially schizophrenia) among young, male, bachelor farmers" (286). She provides the following example:

> Called to his face a wretched, unfortunate, ungainly soul, a leftover, miserable remnant of flesh, the "old cow's calf" is caught in a classic double-bind in which he is damned if he does, and damned if he doesn't. The parent can be observed belittling the runt for trying to put himself ahead, and then with the same breath chiding him for not being more aggressive and achievement oriented like his older brothers. A double-binding predicament is also implicit in the lastborn son's limited choice of alternatives, neither of which is satisfactory. The boy can leave home and "abandon" his parents, but terrible guilt and possibly his mother's curse will follow him ever after ("Johnny, you're the last one we have left!"). Or he can gracefully accept the assigned role of stay-at-home bachelor farmer and parent caretaker but in

this case he will have to face the cruel ridicule and mocking pity of parents and neighbours who will remind him ever after that he is an inadequate adult, forever a "boy-o," and never a man. (294)

Scheper-Hughes (2001) draws heavily on Bateson's (1972) double-bind theory of dysfunctional family communications to first describe the shocking way captive sons are consigned to permanent celibacy, involuntary poverty, obedience, and exploitation (see also Bateson et al. 1956). Second, she attributes these family and community crises, occurring amidst the loss of village life, to the unstoppable forces of urbanization, industrialization, and mass out-migration following Ireland's entry into the Common Market. Third, the book gestures back to an older anthropological tradition (Benedict, Mead, Lévi-Strauss, et al.) and its nostalgia for vanishing cultures. "Traditional culture has become unadaptive, and the newly emerging cultural forms as yet lack integration" (297), she writes, and the result of the dreadful march of progress is the tragedy of schizophrenia and suicide.

Due to her exposure of intimate family secrets and her damning portrayals, Scheper-Hughes was finally rejected by villagers of "Ballybran." She addresses this painful consequence in the 2001 edition of her book. Nonetheless, her book provokes some difficult questions. What responsibility does the anthropologist have to reconcile exposing the darker sides of human culture with people's desires these be kept hidden? Is Scheper-Hughes willfully selective with her data to suit the dominant theory of the day? If schizophrenia is willfully inflicted by parents, as she claims, how can these sons manage their caretaking duties? Certainly some activist groups have successfully changed the idea that schizophrenia is caused by parents (see Chapter 1), as well as the idea that hearing voices is a life sentence.

For example, the international Hearing Voices Movement was founded in 1987. This "post-psychiatric" organization views auditory hallucinations as an aspect of human difference and *not* a mental health problem. It asserts that many people cope with their voices, live successfully, and find their voices life-enhancing. It is not voices per se, but people's relationship with their voices, and social prejudices, that are problematic (see also Luhrmann 2012b). Where voices do cause mental distress, the movement develops interventions for practitioners. This radical assertion, which may increase opportunities for patients to discover their own resilience, should be taken seriously by patients, psychiatrists, and anthropologists.

To conclude, following the decline of psychoanalysis in psychiatry, anthropological research into the "big three" highlights some diverse individual and social relationships of meaning. In unpacking reductionist divisions between mania and depression, and madness and sanity, anthropologists have refuted Kraepelin's early catastrophic prognosis. They have also revealed the limits of psychiatry, and of local healers and traditional medicine, to understand and treat major forms of mental illness. They have taken the position of healer, critic, moral relativist, and mouthpiece of intellectual fashion with sometimes brilliant, sometimes harmful, consequences. Ultimately, there are many theories but no conclusive explanation of the "big three" as the most commonly diagnosed mental disorders. Therefore, perhaps the best contribution anthropologists can make is to keep in view the complexity and ambiguity of human behavior in their analyses, and to keep at play the rich fabric of political, biomedical, mystical, community, and familial valences.

Discussion and Activities

Given that many psychiatrists outside the United States believe childhood bipolar disorder is a false epidemic and does not exist, why are increasing numbers of American children being diagnosed with this and other disorders (e.g., obsessive-compulsive disorder, antisocial personality disorder, ADHD)?

Do "fashions" for particular disorders increase prevalence rates? Discuss and include examples.

Women's rates of depression are higher than men's globally, whereas men experience higher rates of alcohol abuse and antisocial behavior. Discuss in relation to socio-economic aspects, social position, family responsibilities, and specific mental health risks. Are gender differences in depression an artifact—that is, due to women's greater reporting of symptoms than men's?

How is the Hearing Voices Movement, which is very active in Europe, the United States, and Australia, active in confronting biomedical approaches to treating schizophrenia?

How might ethnographic texts and films serve mental health service providers, educators, policy makers, and mental health service users' family members?

Either review online tests, blogs, and chat forums for sufferers of bipolar disorder and examine the construction of common experience, meaning, and public consensus, or review chat forums on any of the following single drugs prescribed for depression: Prozac, Zoloft, Celexa, or Effexor. Discuss the creation of "common" understandings.

Additional Films and Readings

Films

Bethel: Community and Schizophrenia in Northern Japan. 2013. Film (DVD). Directed by Karen Nakamura.

Ritual Burdens. 2011. Directed by Robert Lemelson. Afflictions: Culture and Mental Illness in Indonesia. Anthropology and Psychiatry Film Series. Watertown, MA: Documentary Educational Resources.

When Medicine Got It Wrong. 2009. Directed by Katie Cadigan and Laura Murray. Watertown, MA: Documentary Educational Resources.

Readings

Davison, Kenneth. 2006. "Historical Aspects of Mood Disorders." *Psychiatry* 5: 115–18.

Kernberg, Otto. 1967. "Borderline Personality Organization." *Journal of the American Psychoanalytic Association* 15: 641–85.

Mains, Daniel. 2015. "Reconnecting Hope: *Khat* Consumption, Time, and Mental Well-Being among Unemployed Young Men in Jimma, Ethiopia." In *Global Mental Health: Anthropological Perspectives*, edited by Brandon Kohrt and Emily Mendenhall, 87–102. Walnut Creek, CA: Left Coast Press.

Mendenhall, Emily. 2015. "The 'Cost' of Health Care: Poverty, Depression, and Diabetes among Mexican Immigrants in the United States." In *Global Mental Health: Anthropological Perspectives*, edited by Brandon Kohrt and Emily Mendenhall, 205–20. Walnut Creek, CA: Left Coast Press.

Myers, Neely. 2015. "Shared Humanity among Non-specialist Peer Care Providers for Persons Living with Psychosis: Implications for Global Mental Health." In *Global Mental Health: Anthropological Perspectives*, edited by Brandon Kohrt and Emily Mendenhall, 325–40. Walnut Creek, CA: Left Coast Press.

O'Nell, Teresa. 1998. *Disciplined Hearts: History, Identity and Depression in an American Indian Community*. Berkeley: University of California Press.

CHAPTER 6

GLOBALIZATION, GLOBAL CULTURE, AND GLOBAL MENTAL HEALTH

This chapter examines ways mental disorders are dispersed across the globe. It examines global mental health agendas, for example the Movement for Global Mental Health (MGMH). Global mental health is an international political issue shaped by institutional power, global forces, local experiences, and linkages of structural political and racialized violence. Anthropologists have questioned its core aim to increase access to psychological and psychiatric treatments to address global health inequalities (Kohrt and Mendenhall 2015; Patel et al. 2013; Summerfield 2012). This aim involves a key paradox: while MGMH advocates seek to scale-up access to psychiatry and its treatments in the Global South, these treatments are coming under increased criticism in the North. Relatedly, the chapter involves a historicized critique of North/South, East/West divides. This includes looking again at anthropology's participation in the violence of colonialism and subsequent ways that disordered politics and multiple forms of violence come to constitute "post-colonial disorders" (Good 2012a; DelVecchio Good et al. 2008).

The chapter raises some important questions. Does globalization mean more mental health problems? In 1957, a report published by Alex Sinclair on the mental health of the indigenes of Papua and New Guinea predicted that high incidences of mental illness would result from the "stress of civilization," especially in cities (quoted in Goddard 2011). Today, anthropologists no longer make assumptions about a culture clash between modern and primitive people. Instead they highlight the increasing psychiatrization of distress, the globalization of biopsychiatry, access to drug treatments as an issue of human rights, the neglect of socio-economic determinants in the focus on individual neuropsychiatric explanations of suffering, and the colonialism of ideas (Farmer et al. 2013; Mills 2013). They question whether cultural differences in illness models are adequately accommodated in the view that cultural variations are simply variations of universal disorders; how to resolve tensions between Western-derived ("etic") approaches and local ("emic") community-based initiatives; whether local healing traditions are erased in the drive to scale-up and standardize mental health services (Bemme, Doerte and D'Souza 2012; 2014; Das and Rao 2012); and whether biopsychiatrization ignores bio*social* determinants (Farmer et al. 2013). Last, should we be thinking about global mental health at all, or local political recovery instead (Fernando 2014)? And who should lead the search for solutions—mental health professionals with their Western ideas and vested interests, or affected communities (Fernando 2014)?

What Is Global Mental Health?

An important development for global mental health was a 2001 WHO report that suggested that over "450 million people worldwide are estimated to be suffering at any given time from some kind of mental or brain disorder" (WHO 2001a: 6). In addition, "14% of the global burden of disease has been attributed to neuropsychiatric disorders due to their chronically disabling nature" (6). Amidst this growing "global burden" of mental disorders, the report stated that over "40% of countries have no mental health policy, and over 30% have no mental health programme" (6). Subsequently, in 2007 and 2011, a series of articles published in the prestigious medical journal *The Lancet* argued that the treatment of neuropsychiatric disorders is grossly neglected in low- and middle-income countries (LAMICs). These articles launched the Movement for Global Mental Health (MGMH). They suggest there is a clear evidence base indicating an urgent need for scaling-up mental health services in all countries, but especially in LAMICs (Lancet Global Mental Health Group 2007: 87). The mission states that access to mental health care should be improved, and that inequalities in epidemiologically defined mental health outcomes between and within nations should be reduced. The WHO (2008) echoed the call to "address a treatment gap of more than 75% in many countries with low and lower middle incomes" (4), reiterating its endorsement of mental disorders as "truly universal ... they have a physical basis in the brain ... they can affect everyone, everywhere" (WHO 2001b: 22). "Access" is framed as a pressing moral imperative, and affordable medications as basic human rights (Mills 2013: 452; Patel, Boyce et al. 2011: 1442). Although the *Lancet* series was the catalyst for the "new" global mental health, other developments were crucial for its implementation. These included the Mental Health Gap Action Programme (mhGAP) and the Grand Challenges in Global Mental Initiative (GCIGMH) (Collins et al. 2011; Patel, Belkin et al. 2013).

These recommendations are built on the 2001 World Health Report noted above, which states "there can be no health without mental health," eliding physical and mental illness as biomedical problems with drug-based solutions. Since 1977, the WHO Action Programme on Essential Drugs has incorporated pharmaceuticals for mental health into world health agendas. In 2000, the UN International Covenant on Economic, Social and Cultural Rights stated its aim was "to provide essential drugs, as from time to time defined under the WHO Action Programme on Essential Drugs." The WHO report (2001b) argued that advances in neuroscience now mean the majority of psychiatric disorders can be successfully treated with pharmacological treatments. These should be integrated into primary care worldwide. The United Nations Millennium Development Goals and Beyond (2015) target global inequalities in health and, in cooperation with pharmaceutical companies, "aim to provide access to affordable essential drugs in developing countries" (Target 8E). The MGMH thus has the continued support of the world's largest healthcare funders and institutions.

Anthropologists have both challenged and advanced understandings of globalized connections between physical and mental health (Patel and Kleinman 2003). On the one hand, they highlight how underdevelopment, conflict, and poverty are seen in global health terms to *cause* mental disorders. Consequently, political, economic, and social forces driving suffering become framed as individual mental disease. On the other hand, the global distribution of psychiatric knowledge via the WHO leads classificatory and diagnostic techniques to homogenize categories of distress from around the world, creates new markets for the pharmaceutical industry, and promotes the globalization of "American" forms of suffering (Watters 2011).

Some Key Critiques

Some prominent critiques have been directed at global mental health (GMH) agendas, many from McGill's Division of Social and Transcultural Psychiatry. First are criticisms directed at the biomedical model of psychiatry and the overprescription of psychiatric medication (Timimi 2008). These suggest that the biomedical model fails to provide convincing evidence for the neural or chemical imbalances claimed to cause most psychiatric disorders, and that treatments are ineffective (Moncrieff, Cohen, and Mason 2009: 101). They highlight the psychiatrization of distress, the nondemocratic development of diagnosis and treatment, and the lack of consensus on treatment approaches and on what constitutes evidence of effectiveness (Becker et al. 2013). Others, for example the Grand Challenges in Global Mental Health Initiative, challenge claims that "depression, anxiety disorders, schizophrenia, bipolar disorders, alcohol and drug use disorders, mental disorders of childhood, migraines, dementias, and epilepsy" are primary neurological conditions in the "global disease burden" (National Institute of Mental Health 2010). Claims for biological universality might be compelling if a straightforward biological cause exists, but this only applies to a few psychiatric categories and—as we have discussed—not to schizophrenia, bipolar disorder, depression, and many other commonly diagnosed disorders (Summerfield 2008). Yet vast profit-making opportunities for pharmaceutical companies result in "disease-mongering," overdiagnosis, unnecessary tests and treatments, and wasted resources (Clark 2014: 4). Moreover, studies on the effectiveness of antidepressants, benzodiazepines, and antipsychotics have been found to be incomplete, flawed, contestable, manipulated, and falsified (Healy, Mangin, and Antonuccio 2013; Moncrieff, Cohen, and Mason 2009). Fernando (2011) asks ironically, "Has psychiatry been such a success here (in high-income countries) to entitle us to export it all over the world" (22)?

The second critique of GMH agendas is epitomized in the question, Whose knowledge counts (Bemme and D'Souza 2014: 863)? In the GMH literature, disorders are universally defined and treated without regard for views people in various cultural contexts have about their problems (Summerfield 2008: 2012). The key message of GMH agendas is that mental suffering can be treated with medication and supplemented where necessary by Western talking treatments, regardless of cultural context (Ingelby 2014). The objective is stated as: "The mhGAP guidelines should become the standard approach for all countries and health sectors; irrational and inappropriate interventions should be discouraged and weeded out" (Patel, Boyce et al. 2011: 1442). This means LAMIC populations will inevitably fail to meet the norms imposed by a universalizing global standard—itself a cultural construction. This universalizing move of applying psychiatric classifications globally establishes a hierarchy where high-income countries (HICs) always appear more advanced because the criteria to be met come from these countries (Mills 2013: 32). Notably, the call by GMH agendas for a "universal standard" barely acknowledges the substantial knowledge about the cultural and social origins of mental disturbances developed by medical anthropologists and transcultural psychiatrists over the last half century. It also ignores the plurality of systems people use for alleviating mental distress. For instance, in parts of South Asia, "health pluralism" is the norm (Nichter 1980; Halliburton 2004; Tribe 2007). In Central Sri Lanka this might involve using any combination of Western medicine, ayurvedic medicine, healing rituals, religious *pujas*, astrological consultation, fortune-telling, spirit healing, or Buddhist meditation (Vogt 1999, quoted in Fernando 2014).

Third, GMH interventions for "individual" problems neglect socioeconomic factors such as housing, employment, and social networks, and medicalize many social, economic, and political problems (Clark 2014).

Trying to solve complex social problems by delivering better mental health services may suit certain economic and political interests and maintain inequalities and health disparities (Kirmayer and Pederson 2014). Importantly, Kirmayer (2013) stresses we should not idealize the "anticolonial resistance" of LAMICs who have not adopted GMH agendas wholesale. In many countries, inadequate care means that many people psychiatrists would consider severely disturbed are tied up for long periods at home and in institutions; conditions in many indigenous healing centers and psychiatric hospitals are abusive. Drugs that alleviate suffering *should* be made available, where appropriate.

Fourth, the global march of GMH agendas has been justified via a discourse of human rights, and subject to colonial critiques. For example, China Mills's (2014) study of the controversial notion of the "psychotropic childhood" asks the uncomfortable question of whether access to pharmaceutical treatments of mental disorders should be every child's right. By reproducing a picture published in the journal *Nature* of a "mentally ill" child chained to a tree in Somalia and positioning it next to calls by the WHO and the MGMH to increase access to psychiatric medications, Mills interrogates the image of psychiatric drugs as agents that unshackle and break chains (194). Noting that in some countries of the Global North, "mental illness" in children is framed as an "epidemic," with up to eight million children in the United States taking one or more powerful, sometimes harmful, psychotropic drugs, she proposes children's "right to psychiatrization" as a form of colonial violence: "as psychotropic drugs enter children's bodies they may well be one of the deepest and most intrusive forms of colonization" (201). Next, the powerful discourse that mental illness originates in "brain disease," combined with the interweaving of psychiatry, pharmaceuticals, and development in pressures to increase the export of drug treatments from North to South, raises serious questions about the construction of this "right" (201).

Let us examine these issues more specifically in an "epidemic" of farmer suicides in India.

"Harvesting Despair"

Until 1970 in India, cultivation of cotton and soybean crops relied on indigenous seed varieties with minimal cost to farmers. After 1970 (the advent of the Green Revolution in India), hybrid seed varieties were produced and marketed by private companies, pushing up prices. In 2004 the company Monsanto began selling Bt cotton seeds in India, after the World Trade Organization (WTO) forced India to adopt seed patenting. Monsanto subsequently monopolized the market. It advertised Bt cotton seeds heavily to illiterate farmers, promising high yields and profits. Yet

Monsanto failed to explain that its seeds required expensive pesticides and needed fertilizing and watering according to precise timetables. This was impractical for farmers who lacked irrigation systems and depended on unpredictable rainfall. As farmers rushed to buy Bt cotton seeds, the conventional seed they previously used, requiring only cow-dung fertilizer, swiftly disappeared from many communities. Farmers borrowed money at extortionate rates. As they were highly vulnerable to crop failures and fluctuating crop prices in the global market, many sold their land at a loss and became destitute. Shockingly high rates of farmer suicides followed. The story is poignantly captured in the film *Bitter Seeds* (2011), whose protagonist, a young girl named Manjusha, goes looking for answers after her father's suicide.

China Mills (2013) examines Indian farmer suicides in Vidarbha, located in the Indian state of Maharashtra, in her book *Decolonizing Global Mental Health* (2013), specifically Chapter 2, "Harvesting Despair: Suicide Notes to the State and Psychotropics in the Post" (35–50). (The title "Harvesting Despair" is borrowed from the book with the same name published by Perspectives Group in 2009.) She questions how political rationales work in the ways that people's distress resulting from a socio-economic and agrarian crisis becomes reconfigured as individual mental illness (35). Vidarbha is known for the cultivation of cotton and soybean, and as a suicide district. From June to September 2008 one suicide was recorded every eight hours. In 2007 over 4,000 farmers committed suicide in Maharashtra, almost four times the national average. In areas like Vidarbha, the rate was nearly ten times more, around 53 in every 100,000 farmers. The Indian government emphasized genetic factors that could have made individuals in Vidarbha more prone to suicidal tendencies and called for a scaling-up of psychiatric interventions (37). These interventions diverted attention away from the state's role in instituting deadly economic reforms and reduced the reasons for suicide to the individual body and mind (37). The GMH response proposed to improve medical care for pesticide poisoning in LAMICs, alongside access to antidepressants. The pattern was circular. Preventing farmer suicides led to profitable pharmaceutical interventions, which perpetuated deadly agrarian reforms and farmers' suffering (50).

Anindya Das (2011: 23) links farmers' suicides directly to agricultural trade liberalization and the influence of the WTO. Others emphasize neoliberal agricultural policy reforms and the chronic stresses arising from the debts farmers incur, *not* pre-existing mental illnesses. Suicide might also describe a desperate form of communication. For example, an independent research study of farmers' suicide notes found that many directly accused the prime minister and the Indian state of betrayal; it called for the problem to be seen as farmers' homicides, not farmers' suicides (Perspectives Group 2009). Other critics question if these problems are even correctly formulated. That is, is it "appropriate to frame the suicide of farmers in rural India or alcoholism and drug addiction in the slums of big cities in terms of neuropsychiatric disorders? Should not the social, economic, and political roots of these problems be investigated and tackled first" (Ingelby 2014: 335)? Nor are farmers' suicides exclusive to India. Around 300,000 farmer deaths a year due to self-poisoning with pesticides have been estimated to occur in the Asia-Pacific region alone (Gunnell and Eddleston 2003).

Global Mental Health in a Colonial Context

To consider a critique of the origins of global mental health in colonialism, let's next consider questions such as Whose knowledge counts? and Who should lead interventions? Jeremy Greene and colleagues (2013) trace the history of global mental health from "colonial medicine," through the nineteenth-century science associated with imperial rule and colonization, to associated forms of "tropical medicine" and "missionary medicine," to "international health," "global health," and finally "global mental health" (33–73). They give examples of ways colonial projects damaged the health of indigenous populations, for example the opium trade established between India and China (36), and of anthropologists who introduced new diseases to tribal communities (see controversies surrounding Napoleon Chagnon's study of the Yanomamo). Colonial medicine was additionally used for intelligence purposes (38). It still is. In 2011 the CIA used fake polio vaccination programs in Pakistan in its counterterrorism activities. This led to a blanket refusal by rural community leaders to allow "foreign" workers to administer polio vaccines, despite assurances from the CIA they would discontinue the practice.

After World War II, with the decline of empires, relationships between former colonizers and colonized became reorganized around languages of "development." These practices were still deeply rooted in colonial disparities: now the world's wealthiest nations could "help" the world's poorest (Greene et al. 2013: 60). In 1948, the WHO was formed as a global unified health body and worked with governments to tackle "international health" crises. By 2010, the WHO had 193 member countries. In 1978, an important international conference in Alma-Ata in Kazakhstan gained support for the goal of universal health. In the 1980s, these ideals were profoundly transformed in the new economic context of structural adjustment programs, declining public investment, and the rise of neoliberalism. Economic forces and market-based approaches reshaped the institutional development of key global health bureaucracies, including the WHO, the United Nations Children's Fund (UNICEF), the International Monetary Fund (IMF), and the World Bank (Basilico et al. 2013: 86). Today, advocates of global health equity are increasingly opposing the "health-as-commodity" model in favor of returning to the principles of Alma-Ata.

Many anthropologists critique global mental health agendas within the legacy of the growth of colonial medicine alongside the growth of empires, globalization, and a crude geography based on first, second, or third worlds (Farmer et al. 2013: xii). Critical and postcolonial authors also highlight the imperial subjugation of non-European peoples, the dominance of Western imperial political and economic power (Said 1993), and powerful racialized constructions that subordinate non-Western Others to the authority of "Western humanism" (Spivak 1988). Chapter 2 reflected on some anthropological critiques of humanitarianism as an industry and ideology. Fassin's (2007) Foucauldian critique of a "moral politics of compassion" emphasizes unequal, contradictory power relations between victims and spectators, those who choose to intervene and those who must, and victims deemed worthy of assistance or not (519). These inequalities underpin the logic of "humanitarian reason" (Fassin 2011).

Anthropologists have long questioned the ways that power, diverse actors' intentions, and bald profiteering can be challenged and transformed. This may mean retaining local strategies and understandings over global mental health agendas and pharmaceutical treatments—especially where the latter and psychiatrists are not available, and indeed even where they are (for some interesting discussion, see Patel 2003; Patel et al. 2013). Some very interesting evidence comes from work conducted with poor Indians in rural settings where, collaborating with community care workers, researchers found that experts could use local strategies and idioms of distress with basic social support and psychological methods to treat people with depression, with about the same results as might be found in a psychiatric clinic (Chowdhary et al. 2016). This finding is very important with respect to populations underserved by psychiatrists and psychologists, and by the movement for global mental health equity. To elaborate, to address the high incidence of people with depression who do not receive effective medical and psychological treatments (the "treatment gap"), these researchers systematically developed a short-term psychological treatment of patients with severe depression delivered by lay counselors in primary care, labeled the Healthy Activity Program. They identified potential treatment strategies from the Indian and local context that could map global models, evaluated their feasibility for local delivery, and developed a treatment based on four dimensions: engagement (including psychoeducation), activation (activities and physical exercise), need-based strategies (including relaxation and problem-solving), and social integration. The effectiveness of a systematic approach promises well for other mental disorders in other low-resource settings.

One book that does much to redress the neocolonial tendency of GHM thinking, and its tendency to ignore the contribution of anthropology, is Kohrt and Mendenhall's collection *Global Mental Health: Anthropological Perspectives* (2015). This book ploughs the vibrant interface of global mental health, with its programmatic focus on evidence-based interventions—with anthropological debates about psychiatric diagnoses, healing and health systems, and personal and social experiences of mental illness across cultures. Thereby it contributes uniquely to both disciplines. Following a foreword by Vikram Patel, many case studies across a range of high- and low-income countries, including in Haiti, Ethiopia, Mozambique, Liberia, Nicaragua, and the United States, are scrutinized. These are brought together to build an ethnographic approach to the social and structural origins of mental illness in a global context; to addresses treatment approaches in low- and high-income settings and highlight connections between individual country systems and mental health service provisions globally; and to reflect on task-sharing in this multiplex system between specialist and nonspecialist providers. Several studies from this collection appear on the additional Readings lists in this book.

Postcolonial Disorders

Let us turn to reflect on some theorizations of "postcolonial disorders." This term can highlight the legacies of imperialism, colonialism, and slavery in modern cultural formations of mental disorder. We recall how Fanon (1963) argued that mental disorders in French Algeria were caused directly by the dehumanization of colonialism. DelVecchio Good and colleagues (2008) have since developed more sophisticated analyses of political contexts and individual madness in their book *Postcolonial Disorders*. The book unpacks three dimensions to the term, which it suggests can assist anthropologists in exploring how forms of political, social, and mental life coalesce in disordered realities. It also returns us here to Byron Good's (2012a) definition of "disorder," which was discussed in the introduction. That is, "subjectivity" can link "histories of colonialism ... national and global economic and political processes, and the most intimate forms of everyday experience" (2–3). It can be enriched by drawing from postcolonial theorists who have long informed thinking around race, ethnicity, culture, and so on, especially in understanding globalization, neoliberalism, and the political forces that shape subjectivity across the world. Anthropologists of mental disorder can make the term relevant to psychiatry and open up new ways of thinking about health disparities, culturally appropriate psychotherapy, and treatment services (DelVecchio Good et al. 2008: 5). Lastly, the term disorder can encompass the suffering of people who experience severe loss, violence, insecurity, and oppression and provide a way to analyze "social life and subjectivities that reflect, ironically, the establishment of political, moral and epistemic orders through state violence that reproduces disorder" (8).

In their book, DelVecchio Good and colleagues (2008) expand on this approach. The book is dedicated posthumously to Begoña Aretxaga whose essay "Madness and the Politically Real" was influential in introducing ideas from psychoanalysis into theorizations of political terror and madness, particularly ways historical legacies of violence appear in the present as traumatic memory, inherited institutional structures, and unexamined or hidden assumptions (6). Historically, anthropology as a discipline has been antagonistic toward psychoanalysis and particularly skeptical about claims regarding the unconscious. However, many anthropologists have pursued some diverse and fascinating linkages between psychoanalysis and anthropology, and the field of psychoanalytic anthropology is growing steadily (for some diverse, interesting works, see Borneman 2011; Corin 2014; Crapanzano 2006; Denham 2014; Frank and Frank 1991; Good 2012b; Hansen 2012; Mitchell 1974; Moore 2007; Obeyesekere 1990; Paul 1989).

Those readers who feel brave enough to tackle a complex study of culture and psychosis might try Sadeq Rahimi's book *Madness, Meaning and Political Subjectivity in Turkey* (2015). Rahimi combines psychoanalysis, religious Sufi texts, and theories of power and meaning in Turkish politics. Using this framework, he analyzes schizophrenic and delusional experiences among three patients on different psychiatric hospital wards across Istanbul. Rahimi argues that the individual narratives of "Emel," "Senem," and "Ahmet" show how cultural forms are always simultaneously and meaningfully related to contemporary struggles for political power and to historical struggles for power and identity. Rahimi argues strongly for interpreting individual psychotic experience within its historical, cultural, and political contexts. Indeed, he sees these factors as inseparable and provides an important challenge to the universalizing tendency of GMH agendas, while also reminding us of the early emphasis on psychoanalysis in psychiatry.

This chapter concludes with a provocative visual study, Lemelson's film *Memory of My Face* (2011). The film concerns one man, Bambang Rujito, diagnosed with schizoaffective disorder, and his experiences of acute psychosis, hospitalization, and recovery in Indonesia. Like all of Lemelson's films in the "Afflictions" series, it is accompanied by a comprehensive study guide. Bambang was a former student of Indonesia's foremost university before he worked on the stock market and then for the Unilever Corporation. His first psychotic breakdown coincided with the economic collapse of the Indonesian stock markets in 1999. Over the next four years, he was hospitalized several times with severe mania combined with delusions and hallucinations. After 2003, Bambang taught English to schoolchildren for a while, but to avoid triggering his illness he now does the domestic work while his wife supports the family. He takes support from his interfaith religious community, which suits his skill at holding many different ideas in mind at once—although this characteristic is also more darkly reflected in his manic episodes.

Lemelson shows how ideas about colonialism, postcolonialism, and globalization are reflected in Bambang's experiences of psychosis. He films Bambang in the hospital talking about his life and shows snippets of manic speech that draw frenetically and disjointedly on lyrics from 1980s American pop songs, verses from the Qur'an, the national suffering of 300 years of Dutch colonial rule, the Japanese occupation, Indonesia's violent transition to independence, the 1965 massacre of suspected communists, and the autocratic "colonialist" rule of Suharto. These historical traumas are interwoven with personal references to his father who died when Bambang was young, to a deadly train crash he witnessed as a boy, and to his early life in a village with his aunt after his mother moved to the city for work. These globalized features are demonstrated in the following quote, taken from the film's study guide:

> Ambivalence about colonialism, globalization, and his own subject position seems to trigger interpenetrating affects that cycle quickly for Bambang. On the one hand, he enacts a fascinating metonymic transfer of mental illness, saying to anthropologist, psychologist, and Caucasian filmmaker Robert Lemelson "bye-bye Schizophrenia," symbolically relocating pathology onto the surrogate colonizing body in order to banish it. Yet, at the same time, Bambang gleefully welcomes the opportunity to practice his English and engage in the exchange, performing his broad cosmopolitan knowledge that just might have the power to change him from being "schizoaffective" to being "effective." In his rapidly shifting thoughts, that dart from memory to media story and back again, Bambang negotiates the euphoria and grief of a globalized subjectivity, diagnosing this condition with yet another poignant pun: "The most disturbed patient, his name is 'The World.'" (Tucker and Lemelson 2011: 27)

To conclude, this chapter showed continuities between colonialism and global mental health agendas. It also revealed how shifting meanings and fissures in colonial and postcolonial power can create critical institutional and social change. Many activists have resisted the global health imperium, the biopsychiatric discourse of the universality of mental suffering, and the elision of pharmaceutical treatments with principles of liberty, equity, and human rights. Anthropologists have challenged ways pharmaceuticals for mental health problems are marketed in a global setting, and the profiteering of multinationals bears on the difficulty (impossibility even) of addressing the social causes of distress. They have worked hard to retain intellectual critique without compromising action to help alleviate people's suffering. Worryingly, they highlight how drug treatments are producing profound changes to ways of being human, especially where young children are increasingly receiving pharmaceutical treatments for multiple diagnoses.

Discussion and Activities

The globalization of psychiatry means more people are likely to recover from mental illness but also to be diagnosed. Discuss.

How does the Movement for Global Mental Health equate the scaling-up of psychiatric treatments in low- and middle-income countries with human rights?

There is a danger that in advocating the scaling-up of psychiatric medications in the Global South, the Movement for Global Mental Health frames complex psychosocial problems as individual problems of mental illness. Discuss the positive and negative consequences of this statement.

Define the following terms: psychiatrization; depsychiatrization; medicalization of distress; pathologization; psychologization.

What are the main critiques of Global Mental Health agendas?

American society is witnessing an increase in the prevalence of childhood psychiatric disorders (and children receiving multiple psychiatric diagnoses). What factors are influencing this trend?

Is it possible to retain intellectual debates around colonialism and overmedication without these becoming reasons not to treat people suffering genuine distress?

Additional Films and Readings

Films

America's Medicated Kids. 2010. Directed by Louis Theroux. BBC Productions.

The Battle of Algiers. 1966. Directed by Gillo Pontecorvo. Casbah Film.

Bitter Seeds. 2011. Directed by Micha Peled. San Francisco: Teddy Bear Films.

Memory of My Face. 2011. Directed by Robert Lemelson. Afflictions: Culture and Mental Illness in Indonesia. Anthropology and Psychiatry Film Series. Watertown, MA: Documentary Educational Resources.

Online Resources

Mental Health Gap Action Programme (mhGAP), Launch Video, https://www.youtube.com/watch?v=L8iRjEOH4Ic

Vikram Patel, "Why Mental Health Matters to Global Health," McGill (Canada) University Lecture, https://www.youtube.com/watch?v=rZ9FxFHgVzU

Derek Summerfield, "Against Global Mental Health," McGill (Canada) University Lecture, https://www.youtube.com/watch?v=DOZ5wKvUZXI

Readings

Béhague, Dominique. 2016. "Psychiatry, Bio-epistemes and the Making of Adolescence in Southern Brazil." *História Ciências Saúde-Manguinhos* 23: 13–154.

Desjarlais, Robert, Leon Eisenberg, Byron Good, and Arthur Kleinman. 1995. *World Mental Health: Problems and Priorities in Low-Income Countries.* Oxford: Oxford University Press.

Etkind, Alexander. 2009 "Post-Soviet Hauntology: Cultural Memory of the Soviet Terror." *Constellations: An International Journal of Critical and Democratic Theory* 16: 182–200.

Fassin, Didier. 2007. "Humanitarianism as a Politics of Life." *Public Culture* 19: 499–520.

Fernando, Suman. 2010. *Mental Health, Race and Culture.* 3rd ed. Basingstoke, UK: Palgrave Macmillan.

Kohrt, Brandon, and Emily Menenhall. 2015. "Introduction." In *Global Mental Health: Anthropological Perspectives*, edited by Brandon Kohrt and Emily Mendenhall, 13–18. Walnut Creek, CA: Left Coast Press.

Mendenhall, Emily, and Brandon Kohrt. 2015. "Anthropological Methods in Global Mental Health Research." In *Global Mental Health: Anthropological Perspectives*, edited by Brandon Kohrt and Emily Mendenhall, 37–50. Walnut Creek, CA: Left Coast Press.

Rylko-Bauer, Barbara, Linda Whiteford, and Paul Farmer, eds. 2009. *Global Health in Times of Violence.* Santa Fe: SAR Press.

Taussig, Michael. 1992. *The Nervous System.* New York: Routledge.

Watters, Ethan. 2011. *Crazy Like Us: The Globalization of the American Psyche.* New York: Free Press.

CHAPTER 7

DRUGS, GOD, AND TALKING: SHAPING NEW "ORDERS" OUT OF "DISORDER"

This chapter shifts to ideas of recovery, and to ways different treatment techniques shape new "orders" out of "disordered" realities. First, it outlines ways the proliferating use of prescription drugs, and illegal drugs, have shaped not as much "cures" as new ways of being human, alongside perceptions of ourselves as inherently and permanently ill (Dumit 2012). It proceeds to reflect on research that has found religious and spiritual practice can also significantly improve mental health outcomes (Dein and Littlewood 2007; Dein 2013). Indeed, the institutions of religion and psychiatry share several common trajectories. Then the chapter returns to the theme of subjectivity and language. The decline in psychoanalytic psychiatry means that whereas psychiatrists used to commonly talk to people with schizophrenia about their voices, they are now more likely prescribe medications to suppress them. Relatedly, the chapter examines "talking cures" as a mode of anthropological representation and also a therapeutic tool. It asks how anthropologists' studies in language, writing, and film are interwoven into processes of recovery and healing. Importantly, recovery does not necessarily follow treatment. Indeed, many forms of treatment perpetuate the very forms of "craziness" they aim to alleviate.

Drug "Believers"

Has the idea of drug cures become an anachronism, a thing of the past? Big Pharma self-evidently means big money. Dumit (2012) notes that pharmaceutical sales reached about US$880 billion in 2011, with steady growth rates predicted for subsequent years (18). Investments in individual health, particularly treatments of acute symptoms that end when symptoms are suppressed, have now given way to treating health as a mass, future-oriented, pharmaceutical-oriented aggregate of potentially chronic health *risks* whose management requires that (prospective) patients take "Drugs for Life." Adding increasing medications to reduce multiple levels of risk produces what Dumit calls "surplus health" (17) and thereby relegates the idea of drug "cures" to the past. This process is exacerbated by what Dumit identifies as parallel processes of "depsychiatrization" and "psychiatrization" in the marketing of pharmaceutical treatments of mental disorders.

Online "mood disorder" questionnaires and "bipolar awareness commercials" achieve diagnoses "pseudo-democratically" through teaching the public about disease symptoms and by motivating self-diagnosis among people who then seek to convince doctors to prescribe particular drug treatments. Prospective patients must therefore work quite hard to become diagnosed with certain disorders, particularly where diagnoses are required for social security or insurance payments. Interestingly, Dumit likens the process by which symptoms are transformed into psychiatric conditions to techniques of evangelical witnessing, whereby religious nonbelievers become believers through dialogue, participation, identification, and action (66).

Regarding the life course, psychotropic drugs have demonstrably transformed adolescence for an entire generation. Drugs are now routinely taken by adolescents and young adults to enhance performance, memory, or sharpen the mind (e.g., "designer" drugs, or "study" drugs such as Modafinil), recreationally, or medicinally to control cognitive or brain function. Anderson-Fye and Floersch (2011) argue that increased psychotropic medication use in adolescence has probably allowed many students with mental illnesses who would have been unable to attend university previously to attend now. Late adolescence is common for the first onset of psychiatric disorders, including depression, eating disorders, and major psychoses; these can be exacerbated by the demands of college. Kadison (2005) estimates that 25 to 50 per cent of US college students seen in student counseling centers are taking antidepressants. Mental health problems are also rising among academics who face an increasingly marketized higher education system, greater job insecurity, and constant demand for results and "excellence" (Shaw and Ward 2014).

Accounts of psychotropy and the life course describe multiple ways legal and illegal drugs are used to manage mental distress and the demands of modern life, not just in adolescence but throughout life. A 2014 special issue of *Culture, Medicine, and Psychiatry* dedicated to humanness and modern psychotropy includes articles about adolescents receiving drug treatment (buprenorphine) for opiate dependency in the United States; the deep infiltration of psychopharmaceuticals into formal and informal pharmaceutical markets in India; ways new diagnostic technologies have now configured "pre-Alzheimer's patients"; the sharp rise in polypharmacy (taking multiple medications) in the United States; and ways female personhood in India is located at a series of critical junctures involving pharmaceuticals, drugs of vice, independence, and destitution.

Why are some drugs sanctioned for clinical use while others with demonstrated ameliorative effects are not? Let us consider this question in light of the revival of interest in the role of hallucinogens in alleviating mental disorder. Anthropologists have widely studied the role hallucinogenic drugs play in shamanic rituals, medicine, and healing in traditional cultures, including the use of mescaline, ayahuasca, and peyote to gain self-enlightenment and personal insights and to enhance mood and resilience in Amazonian and Andean cultures; in Satanic practices and witchcraft in pre-Victorian Britain; and in contemporary church ceremonies in Brazil (Sessa 2012). We might also learn from studies from the mid-twentieth century that "cured" alcoholism and mental disorders with hallucinogenic drugs.

A 2014 special issue of *The Psychologist* examines the use of "classic" hallucinogens in research, popular culture, and therapy, namely psilocybin (magic mushrooms), dimethyltryptamine (DMT) (the major hallucinogen in ayahuasca), and the synthetic drug LSD (see Bell 2014). Among the studies, Carhart-Harris, Kaelen, and Nutt (2014) argue that experiences of ego-disintegration associated with hallucinogenic states might be used to investigate the neurobiological basis of self-awareness and have utility for treating obsessive-compulsive disorder, addiction, and similar problems characterized by entrenched thought patterns (664). Abraham (2014) examines hallucinogen persisting perception disorder (HPPD) ("when the trip doesn't end"). Perhaps behavioral or pharmacological treatments of HPPD that can rebuild the brain's inhibitory circuitry might help other psychological conditions. Costandi (2014) revisits the work of Humphrey Osmond, a British psychiatrist who pioneered LSD treatments of alcoholism and mental disorders and who originally coined the term psychedelic, meaning "mind-manifesting" (714). Osmond proposed that mescaline produced similar effects to symptoms of schizophrenia. In 1950, Osmond and Albert Hoffer treated alcoholics with LSD. Their work led the British psychiatrist Sandison to open the world's first LSD therapy clinic in 1953 to treat patients with neurosis and schizophrenia. Recent clinical trials using psilocybin, ketamine, and MDMA ("drugs of abuse") have found positive benefits for depression and mood disorders (715). Yet, in the 1960s, LSD was considered a major social threat (Nutt 2014: 659). In 1962, LSD, psilocybin, and DMT were banned in the US. This was followed by a global ban under the 1971 UN drug conventions. Nutt (2014) cites a recent meta-analysis of old clinical trials that found LSD as effective as any other treatment of alcoholism (659). Given that neuroscience technologies (PET, MRI) can advance understandings of how antipsychotic agents work on psychosis,

Nutt argues, "the failure of the scientific community, particularly neuro-scientists, to protest the denial of research on hallucinogens is one of the most disturbing failures of science leadership in the past century" (660).

Confinement and Freedom

The idea that drugs can "open" new areas of the brain mirrors discourses of entry into other worlds and into "miracles" of medical and religious heal-ing. In the treatment of lunatics in eighteenth-century France, Foucault, in *History of Madness* (2006), argues that the asylum largely replaced reli-gion, taking on its moral work and becoming "thus a religious domain stripped of religion, a domain of pure morality and ethical uniformity" (493). Subsequently, psychiatrists such as Pinel, Tuke, and later Charcot and Freud, introduced humanitarian reforms and medical advances into the treatment of the violently insane. This authorized new contacts between doctors and patients, with the result that "mental illness, with all the con-notations that are familiar with us today, then became possible" (504). In the UK, the 1845 Lunacy Act likewise transformed the criminally insane into psychiatric patients. By 1902, lunacy rates had doubled.

Foucault (2006) writes, "It is a curious paradox to see medical practice enter the uncertain domain of the quasi-miraculous just as the science of mental illness was trying to assume a sense of positivity.... As positivism imposed itself on medicine, and above all psychiatry, the practice became more obscure, the power of the psychiatrist more miraculous" (507–08). Thereafter, nineteenth-century psychiatry converged on the mystical power and judgment of the doctor—particularly in Freud, "who took seriously the doctor-patient couple, and freed the patient from the asylum but confined him to the essential character of asylum existence in the psychoanalytic situation" (510).

Foucault (2006) brilliantly details how changing medical truths shifted prescribed treatments of madness from imprisonment to experimental hypnosis, electroshock, and other physical punishments, including frontal lobotomies and leucotomies, to psychoanalysis and the subsequent miracle drug treatments of psychiatry. Some continuities between punitive asylum treatments and modern antipsychotic drugs were also evident. Leader (2011) reflects on Metrazol's use as a convulsion therapy for schizophrenia in the 1930s. Metrazol produced decreased emotional depth, decreased capacity for self-observation, and social withdrawal; that is, quieter, more compliant patients. Given psychotherapy with psychotic subjects is generally long and difficult, Leader argues that such brain-numbing drug regimens—like earlier insulin coma and shock treatments—might describe an unconscious punishment for not getting better (24).

Certainly, the most demonized groups in many societies are sequestered, imprisoned, or even forcibly enrolled in brutal inmate treatment programs.

In his study of sexual offender treatment in Canada, Waldram (2012: 13) argues that the punitive, aggressively delivered treatment of recalcitrant, reluctant, and difficult patients benefits those in charge more than patients themselves. Waldram (2014) is also highly critical of Indigenous "healing programs" in Canadian prisons that address "historical trauma" by encouraging individuals to take personal responsibility for the failure of traditional and government services to deal with the distress of colonialism.

After the 1960s, mass biomedicine resulted in many national psychiatric reforms. These shifted treatment from the asylum, and prison, to outpatient settings. Anthropologists documented many continuities between experiences of dependency, chronic helplessness, and disempowerment among both psychiatric inpatients and "clients" in community care (Brodwin 2013; Davis 2012; Luhrmann 2001). As has been noted, care conditions can sometimes make mental disorder self-reproducing.

Estroff's book *Making It Crazy* (1981) is an interesting earlier example that links the shift toward the deinstitutionalization of severely mentally disturbed patients in American society to social, cultural, and professional ideals that value personal freedom and happiness over confinement and dependence. She shows how, as self-identified or other-identified "crazy people," deinstitutionalized psychiatric clients within the US are enmeshed in systems where "crazy" identities become the means to survive. Staff "exist mainly as markers for differentness or sameness in clients' eyes" (38), not as agents for therapeutic change. Staff-client interactions maintain, rather than eliminate, craziness. "Craziness" has multilayered meanings, bearing on psychiatric symptoms but also on the "processes and factors [that], while intending alleviation of psychiatric disorders and suffering, may be perversely stabilizing, maintaining and perpetuating them" (39). Estroff argues that psychiatric treatments pathologize and may sustain chronic problems in living and being (257). She warns about increasing numbers of people with chronic problems living in the community, as medical advances make it possible to save more lives, but diagnoses of craziness produce the need to maintain craziness (254).

The shifting of treatment to outpatient settings can also place mental health workers in impossible work situations. Paul Brodwin's book *Everyday Ethics* (2013) provides a powerful critique of the ethical dilemmas facing community psychiatrists in the United States. Brodwin shows that psychiatrists criticize the coercion and forced dependency built into frontline care systems, and the chronic challenges these pose to their desires to be competent, compassionate advocates, yet their difficult work conditions mean they also justify their use of extreme power in the face of loud opposition from clients.

Indeed, several social movements have worked hard to improve mental health care conditions and innovate alternatives within the available systems.

These include patient/client/survivor movements, peer-led therapy, "mad pride," and the "recovery" paradigm in mental health provision. All are important cultural aspects of contemporary mental health care in many settings and increasingly the object of anthropological inquiry. "Mad pride" is a global movement that positively reclaims terms like "mad" in a similar way gay-rights activists reclaimed the word queer—to improve both public perceptions and users' and politically defined "ex"-users' experiences of mental health services. McLean (2000) tracks how individuals who were dissatisfied with their experiences of mental health care identified as "ex-patients" or "survivors" radically opposed to the medical model's debilitating effects (including disempowerment, dependence, forced treatment, and involuntary commitment) (823). This antipsychiatry stance changed with the advent of deinstitutionalization and private insurance, and individuals subsequently began viewing psychiatry as a consumer choice amidst an array of treatment options they could select from. Yet, while in reality consumerism gives recognition and power to "ex-patients" and "survivors" and provides links to alternative mental health movements, family advocates, and community support programs, the political ideals driving these alternatives are compromised by restricted options and a two-tiered public-private health system (842).

Another compelling example is Neely Laurenzo Myers's book *Recovery's Edge* (2015). Myers interrogates the effects of the Bush Administration's 2004 mandate to reduce care costs and reintegrate individuals with serious mental illnesses as productive working citizens through "recovery-oriented" care. Her fieldsite is Horizons, a massive rehabilitation organization in urban America. Here, care is conceptualized as a "journey" toward work rather than wellness (52), and employment confers recognition and "moral agency" (13). Former patients work tirelessly in Horizon's Peer Empowerment Program to transform traditional treatment models and promote practices of recovery that value people as human beings (75). Yet their efforts conflict with the recovery program's failure to assist individuals overcome structural violence and their demoralizing "catastrophic conditions of everyday survival" (156). Myers urges service providers to rethink the "logic of care" in a way that helps users live with, not necessarily recover from, serious mental illness and avoid the devastating losses (of sanity, intimacy, jobs, and social support) that frequently accompany relapse (157–58).

The above represent good examples of how the unique conditions of the American health insurance system foster particular cultures of value and care. Those interested in reading more deeply on theoretical contributions of institutionalized care might read the edited volume *Face aux Désastres* (2013) by Anne Lovell and colleagues. This collection conjoins anthropology and philosophy in exploring how varied forms of political, social, and mental life are shaped in four studies on "the anthropology of madness."

Lovell's own chapter examines how already vulnerable, sometimes mentally ill, people for whom living ordinary lives is already extraordinarily difficult cope with the disaster of Hurricane Katrina in New Orleans.

One final issue to briefly consider is the potential framing of mental disorder as "disability" or "impairment" and potential conceptual links to disability studies literatures. This would concern how the mentally ill are valued, devalued, and politically enabled by public perceptions of them as deserving of disability rights. Nev Jones and Timothy Kelly (2015), for example, emphasize the need for greater collaboration between disability and mental health activists in a way that can recognize the diverse positions, backgrounds, and experiences that combine under the consumer/survivor/user umbrella while also retaining the power of identity-based coalitions and activism.

God's Healing Power?

We have identified several linkages between the therapeutic promise of pharmaceuticals and of religion—with new meaning for Marx's maxim that religion serves as the opium of the people. The therapeutic relationship between religion and mental illness is thoroughly debated in anthropology (e.g., Dein 2013; Dein and Littlewood 2007, 2011; Dein, Cook, and Koenig 2012; Dura-Vila et al. 2010; Greenberg, Kalian, and Witztum 2010; Leavey 2010; Popovsky 2010; Sorsdahl, Stein, and Flisher 2010). Anthropological studies can permit emic understandings of ways religion and spirituality are culturally constructed and experienced, and of the differences between normative religious experiences and psychopathologic states in religious communities (Dein 2013: 35). In his work with Orthodox Jews, Dein (2010) argues for incorporating existential and religious issues into clinical practice, and he demonstrates associations between greater religiosity and decreased anxiety, decreased post-traumatic stress symptoms, lower reported depression, and greater reported happiness. Luhrmann (2013) similarly found that prayer may contribute to healing in trauma and psychosis. She explores ideas of "symbolic healing" in the effectiveness of a positive relationship with a "good" and "real" God who is believed to have external agency outside the imagination (708). Drawing on fieldwork with homeless psychotic women in Chicago, she found that women experienced lower stress, lower psychiatric vulnerability, and less loneliness following conversations with a God they imagined as loving, vivid, and present (721).

Luhrmann (2012a: xi) questions how "sensible" people can sustain the belief that God has a demonstrable effect in their lives in the face of skeptical observers and their own doubt. She explores how American evangelical Christians cultivate a real, intimate everyday relationship with God through visualizing themselves conversing with a loving God who "talks back." She argues prayer practice is predominantly good for people, whatever the reality of God, and it can help someone vulnerable to madness to keep it at bay (227). She also emphasizes clear differences between voices heard by evangelicals and the auditory hallucinations of psychosis. Voices experienced in psychosis (in schizophrenia, bipolar disorder, depression, trauma, and substance abuse) may mock, intrude, scream, or command people to harm themselves (228). While there may be some overlap between incipient psychosis and hearing God speak, for evangelicals, hearing voices is overridingly a source of solace, resilience, and happiness (248). One of Luhrmann's informants who suffered psychosis described it "like a kind of high of dating someone you loved who loved you" (298). The woman "heard God tell her, audibly, that she would be a 'face of mental illness,' which she took to mean that her experience would allow people who were afraid to feel more confident. The voice seemed very different from the self-condemning voices inside her head that she associated with her illness" (298).

How might turning to God resolve feelings of endless suffering associated with the chronicity model of addiction? This subject concerns Angela Garcia's eloquent ethnography *The Pastoral Clinic* (2010). Garcia asks how addicts can recover when treatment models perceive addiction as a permanent, unending disease (52). She examines some connections between legal and illegal drug use, psychiatry and religion, and chronicity and ideas of a cure in her study of heroin addiction among a Hispanic community in Espanola Valley in New Mexico. She draws on intergenerational field-work among rural families and in a detoxification clinic for addicts. Garcia links the clinic's "purgatorial sensibility" (52), rooted historically in fragile, precarious formations of community and place, to governmental penal and psychiatric apparatuses that offer no respite from violent cultural, personal, and political histories of loss and the harsh geography of "life outside." Rio Grande's landscape is described as a historical site of dispossession—a "graveyard," involving the forced displacement of Hispano settlers in the mid-nineteenth century, legacies of loss in the Vietnam war, neoliberal policies, poverty, and high rates of incarceration. Many of Garcia's informants were expelled from the houses and land they grew up on and live in trailer parks. Heroin use underscores community and family dynamics of connectedness and longing, historical rupture and painful repetition, love and grief (10). Shifting meanings of "inheritance" (*querencia*) between mother–daughter addicts become inscribed into new blood relations and kinship ties that are maintained less through the heritage of land and property than the destructive inheritance and blood ties (including pustules, sores, and scars) of addiction (115). Garcia writes, "The dependencies produced through heroin became part of the relational mix that is kinship, and the circulation of heroin the substance through which care was performed and affective ties ... reaffirmed" (128). She describes how the institutional failures that consigned former heroin addict "Alma" to destructive cycles of addiction and respite were resolved by her turn to a Christian fellowship support group (87): "Perhaps it was in evangelicalism, and the promise of being born again, that Alma was able to envision putting an end to chronicity and seek for herself a true and lasting recovery" (88).

Religion and psychosis purportedly share some common evolutionary trajectories (Dein and Littlewood 2011). However, studies of religion and florid psychosis have received little attention. Offering a fascinating example from Morocco, Stefania Pandolfo (2008) questions how psychosis and internal conflicts are shaped by ideological conflicts between tradition and religion, modernity and postcolonialism. She analyzes the case of one young man, Reda, who is admitted to a psychiatric emergency department accompanied by his mother. She explores how his speech and imagination—which are shaped by the rigid polarized thinking of psychosis—configure a power confrontation between modern psychiatry, *jinn* possession, and Islamic cultural theology. These conflicts occur against the backdrop of the postcolonial state, and they are inscribed onto his body and life. Whereas for Reda, his illiterate mother embodies all the impotence of "tradition," Reda's own passion for foreign literature and critical thought symbolizes the future, modernity, forward movement, and a *way out* of his psychiatric symptoms of persecution. Reda explicitly says, "*Kanharrab b-la littérature*: I escape, save myself with literature" (343). Pandolfo writes,

> At stake is Reda's struggle against the annihilation of himself.
> The theme of persecution and of his "suffering" (*cette souffrance*)
> in the hell of his experience are the negative and tragic
> dimension of this: imprisonment and paralysis, cannibalization,
> estrangement of the self and affirmation of a right to existence by
> refusal of identifications—with his mother, his language, his tradition.
> The theme of Exit—through education, science and reading, and
> later through literature and the Imagination—raises the question of
> freedom. (343)

With her emphasis on power and on the languages in madness, Pandolfo (2008) returns us to Foucault, to the relation of subjectivity and language, and to wider questions concerning ways people have sought recovery via new creative or therapeutic languages of transformation.

Talking Cures

Do words have the power to heal? First, to continue the relation between religious and psychological or psychiatric forms of healing, there is considerable anthropological work on the role of religious rituals in engendering mental health. However, the mental health implications of specific rituals (e.g., Christian rituals such as baptism, the Eucharist, the laying on of hands) has not been widely researched (Dein 2013: 35). It is less common nowadays for people talk to religious healers or to their spiritual leaders who, through the ritual act of confession, might offer them a fresh start. In many societies today, psychotherapists are more widely invested with the healing power of words. The ritual 50-minute psychotherapy session works to change the narrative and phenomenological meanings of a client's life story to make that life more livable. Psychoanalysis has very different foundations from cognitive-behavioral therapies. The former works with ideas about the unconscious, and the latter with conscious beliefs. A course of analytic psychotherapy typically lasts several years, whereas cognitive-behavioral therapy (CBT) treatments and their derivatives are short. They target changes at a surface level of verbalization to improve a client's efficacy in areas of his or her life. The cost-effectiveness of CBT-based treatments means they predominate over psychoanalysis in government-funded referral programs. Nonetheless, the theory and practice of psychotherapy have been adapted in non-Western cultures (for some interesting readings, see Gee and Loewenthal 2011; House and Loewenthal 2009; Littlewood 2009; Kirmayer 2007; Parish 2008).

Cognitive-behavioral therapies involve particular kinds of verbal techniques. These concern Summerson Carr's (2001) study of an American addiction recovery program. She examines why addiction counsellors seek to reconcile drug users' relationship to *language* in order to reconfigure their relationship to drugs. She analyzes everyday interactions between therapists and clients as "semiotic entanglements" (2). Here, therapists work to *script* intensive verbal interactions to appeal to powerful institutional actors; clients work to represent themselves and their problems, and to skillfully use words to access material and symbolic resources (5). This study in linguistic anthropology shows how rituals of speaking and naturalized cultural narratives are put into practice through "semiotic work." By "flipping" unhealthy scripts—that is, learning to verbalize inner states "healthily"—drug users' reconfigure their relationship to drugs and their emergent sobriety.

In addition to talking to therapists and doctors, or to God or priests, are models of recovery designed around writing activities. Writing may comprise a mode of representing personal experience, healing, and recovery (Bollas 2002; Geertz 1988; Bolton et al. 2004; Kleinman 1995), especially where prevailing models hold that mental illness is chronic and lifelong. Community "writing recovery" groups have proliferated across many parts of the globe, encouraging people to cathartically write about their experiences of war, violence, stalking, mental illness, and so on.

Here we turn to an example of a film about a writing project, Richard Robbins's *Operation Homecoming: Writing the Wartime Experience* (2007), involving US veterans from Vietnam, Korea, Iraq, and Afghanistan. The film builds on a project created by the National Endowment for the Arts that collected the writing of soldiers who participated in wars in Iraq and Afghanistan. Through a series of filmed interviews and dramatic readings of veterans' firsthand written accounts, it describes the search by veterans for understanding and efforts to come to terms with their experiences, including their moral dilemmas about killing. The film does much to correct trite claims of personal and political closure, medical and psychological metaphors of triumph over adversity, and of leaving the past behind. It also offers a pessimistic but powerful view of ways that wartime experiences, including severe trauma, might lead veterans to feel impelled to return to war. One of the most distinctive pieces in the film is by Colby Buzzell, who employs the imagery of animation to describe a traumatic street fight that resulted in several deaths, accompanied by illustrations of spent cartridges and flying bullets. Although Buzzell wrote a popular military blog from the frontlines, when he returned home he was puzzled and dejected to find that people reacted to his experiences with disinterest, awkwardness, or had little to offer in response. The following extract, from Buzzell's blog "Men in Black," describes his experience of manning a military vehicle in an ambush in Mosul in Iraq:

(Sgt Vance) asked if I was O.K. I thought about that one for a second and I told him, "I don't know." I told him how I wasn't really in the mood to roll back out for another inning with these guys, and I also told him that I was kinda tripping out about how not everybody that I engaged today had a weapon in their hands. And that I wasn't really too sure about what happened to some of those people. Vance started telling me a little bit about his father, who had been in Vietnam, and who had given him sound advice about situations like this, "Put all the things that bother you, and keep you awake at night, and clog your head up, put all those things in a shoebox, put the lid on it, and deal with it later." Shortly after that they told us to go back to our rooms. I walked back to my room, thanked God, and passed out on my bed. I've put the events of that day in a shoebox, put the lid on it, and haven't opened it since.

Our last example is an ethnographic filmmaking project that was very successful in promoting recovery. This is Lemelson's film *Bird Dancer* (2010a), which forms part of Lemelson's "Afflictions" series. The film features a young Balinese village girl, Gusti Ayu, who suffers from the neuropsychiatric condition of Tourette syndrome. Tolerated, and by turns cruelly mocked, pitied, and ordered by her family to control her tics, her dreams of marriage, employment, independent living, and of living out the roles of a "normal" life are thwarted. She is viewed as a shameful burden on her family, an object of pity in her community, and her life is filled with deep despair. Her encounters with traditional healers involve painful treatments, in one case sexually exploitative. During the course of the film's making, she meets another woman with Tourette syndrome in Bali, whose symptoms are more severe. The experience of this happily married working mother living with the full support of her family is dramatically different. Gusti Ayu is eventually helped with moving to the city and living independently, where she maintains a job and enjoys supportive friendships. In keeping with expectations for a young Balinese woman, it causes her sadness that she remains unmarried. Gusti returns with Lemelson and other people in the film to organize a public screening in the village. Here her struggles receive powerful recognition. This is an example of how long-term ethnographic filmmaking can widen local knowledge, alleviate deep suffering associated with neuropsychiatric illness, and positively transform community and family stigma.

Does all this emphasis on treatments downplay the ways cures occur "naturally," without intervention? Joel Paris and Hailey Zweig-Frank (2001), for example, found 75 per cent of people with borderline personality disorder functioned adaptively by age 40, and 90 per cent recovered by age 50. Alongside many resourceful ways people have resisted hegemonic understandings, for example that hearing voices is symptomatic of pathology, there are studies that link recovery to the life course and that can provide a counterpoint to the pessimistic dominance of biomedical trends, including the rise in geriatric psychiatry.

To conclude, this chapter tracked some of the many ways psychiatry incorporates religious symbolism, and that miracle drugs of science have led our mental health to be defined by pharmaceutical companies served by psychiatrists, not the reverse. While Foucault (2006: 492) might view contemporary treatments doing the job of imprisonment and control previously accorded asylums, he also acknowledged the curative power of religious "truth." Religious belief and practice demonstrably help people cope with chronic illness and offer exits from intolerable pain and perpetual suffering. Drugs and talk therapies work too. At the same time, diagnoses and treatments may force sufferers of mental disorder into self-reproducing modes of behavior and response, which are themselves sources of mental pathology. Finally, therapeutic narratives, expressive writing, and anthropological filmmaking can also be powerful modalities of recovery that can challenge the hegemony of the biomedical disease model of mental disorder.

Discussion and Activities

Why are some treatments successful for some people, but not everyone? To what extent is "recovery" from severe mental illness possible?

How do "writing" or "talking" cures compare with other forms of treatment, for example, prescription drugs? Which would you opt for and why?

How does writing "work" as a therapeutic tool? How does film work as a therapeutic tool? Discuss in relation to Robbins's film about writing and Lemelson's film *Bird Dancer* as an example of anthropological "healing."

Discuss the ethics involved in the proposed marketing of "end-of-life" or "suicide kits" as a luxury item. What restrictions should be posed? Should these kits be legal, illegal, age-restricted? Would you buy one?

Write a short poem about a difficult time in your own life, or about somebody you know or a celebrity figure who has had difficult times in his or her life.

Research training courses for analytic psychotherapy, counseling, cognitive-behavioral therapies, and life coaching. Compare the implications of each regarding cost, duration, and differential access—and for the associated uptake of particular therapies among different social groups.

Additional Films and Readings

Films

Bird Dancer. 2010. Directed by Robert Lemelson. Afflictions: Culture and Mental Illness in Indonesia. Anthropology and Psychiatry Film Series. Watertown, MA: Documentary Educational Resources. See the accompanying study guides for all six of Lemelson's films in this series at http://www.der.org/resources/study-guides.

Kites and Monsters. 2011. Directed by Robert Lemelson. Afflictions: Culture and Mental Illness in Indonesia. Anthropology and Psychiatry Film series. Watertown, MA: Documentary Educational Resources.

Off Label. 2012. Directed by Michael Palmeiri and Donal Mosher. Brooklyn: Filmscience.

Operation Homecoming: Writing the Wartime Experience. 2007. Directed by Richard Robbins. London: The Documentary Group.

Readings

Borneman, Jon. 2015. *Cruel Attachments: The Ritual Rehab of Child Molesters in Germany.* Chicago: University of Chicago Press.

Davis, Elizabeth Anne. 2012. *Bad Souls: Madness and Responsibility in Modern Greece.* Durham, NC: Duke University Press.

Foot, John. 2015. *The Man Who Closed the Asylums: Franco Basaglia and the Revolution in Mental Health Care.* London: Verso.

Frank, Jerome D., and Julia Frank. 1991. *Persuasion and Healing: A Comparative Study of Psychotherapy.* Baltimore: Johns Hopkins University Press.

Friedman, Jack. 2015. "Who Belongs in a Psychiatric Hospital? Post-Socialist Romania in the Age of Globalizing Psychiatry." In *Global Mental Health: Anthropological Perspectives*, edited by Brandon Kohrt and Emily Mendenhall, 191–204. Walnut Creek, CA: Left Coast Press.

Hopper, Kim. 1991. "Some Old Questions for the New Cross-Cultural Psychiatry." *Medical Anthropology Quarterly* 5: 299–330.

Kareem, Jafar, and Roland Littlewood. 1992. *Intercultural Therapy: Themes, Interpretations and Practice*. Oxford: Blackwell.

Kirmayer, Laurence. 2007. "Psychotherapy and the Cultural Concept of the Person." *Transcultural Psychiatry* 44: 232–57.

Langlitz, Nicolas. 2012. *Neuropsychedelia: The Revival of Hallucinogen Research since the Decade of the Brain*. Berkeley: University of California Press.

Seligman, Rebecca. 2014. *Possessing Spirits and Healing Selves: Embodiment and Transformation in an Afro-Brazilian Religion*. New York: Palgrave Macmillan.

Weinstein, Deborah. 2013. *The Pathological Family: Postwar America and the Rise of Family Therapy*. Ithaca, NY: Cornell University Press.

CONCLUSION

Now that we have reached the end of this book, we have almost come full circle, from early biological approaches and psychosurgeries such as leucotomies to the contemporary age of "the brain" and its related treatments. While this book largely concerns contemporary approaches, the history of madness reveals many transformations in understandings of mental disorder. For example, John Locke's "An Essay Concerning Human Understanding" (1690) influenced early French psychiatrists such as Pinel and Tuke, and it shifted ideas about madness from hereditary causes, religious terms of demonic possession, and punishment for sins to those derived from the false association of ideas. In documenting this history, Foucault (2006) is very important. He shows us how the criminally insane became transformed into patients, and how the asylum became a new site of scientific and medical investigation. This more humanitarian approach introduced the potential for change. It also raised new questions about ways madness and sanity might cohabit in the same person. These developed in the eighteenth and nineteenth centuries in early psychiatry's conceptualizations of new "nerve" maladies, through early neurology and ideas of the "nervous system," and later through Freud who investigated problems of neurosis in psychoanalysis. Around the same time, modern conceptions of psychosis were developed by Bleuler, Kraepelin, Wernicke, and others whose work still informs current classifications of the "big three" most commonly diagnosed disorders.

These developments in classical psychiatry occurred alongside large-scale industrialization and modernization. In his 1903 essay "The Metropolis and Mental Life," Georg Simmel ([1903] 2002) argued that the nineteenth-century city offered "man" and his work more liberty, while also demanding that individuals become intensely competitive. The city became seen as a place whose impressions could overload the nervous system—a place where lunacy proliferated. For Simmel, the city stood as a metaphor for the abnormal, dangerous risks residing "within" (society and the mind) the consequences of unchecked urbanization, alien immigration, and modernity.

This book built on such critiques, and it tracked the development of Western psychiatry through various epochs and across the globe. It showed how anthropology furnishes a raft of perspectives on ways grand

and particular dimensions of culture, environments, and biology interact with "disorder." Our culturalist perspectives challenge the old Boasian functionalist view of culture and personality; the individualizing, internalizing epistemic logic (culture) of psychiatric nosology; and the insidious legacy of colonial race politics. Importantly, critiques from anthropology have not all been empty rhetoric. In developing their criticisms of global mental health, and the imperium of Western psychiatry, anthropologists have made important advances in cultural and global psychiatry, including cultural formulation of the DSM-5. In doing so, they have largely disabused the figure of the mad Other of its exoticism, primitivism, distance, abnormality, and characteristics of radical difference. This figure has additionally been brought to live among us in intimate proximity by medics, critical and community psychiatrists, activists, and Big Pharma. While the florid madness that encompasses the extremes of human behavior may be organically distinct, the proximity of "madness" has allowed anthropologists to analyze ways it might also exist in quieter, everyday forms on a continuum of structural, institutional, and symbolic violence that can affect us all. They have been able to investigate interactions of biological (including hereditary and epigenetic) factors and cultural and social etiologies—even if the exact pathways between these various elements have yet to be more explicitly demarcated.

This book engaged in conversations with philosophy, literature, medicine, history, and science. It emphasized continuity in our discipline's historical commitment to uphold internal diversity in its modes of inquiry—while thinking through new ways about the production of mental disorder within historical patterns of power, international politics, and local patterns and languages of suffering. In doing so it revealed rich "insights" into ways anthropologists interpret experiences that are radically different to our own and how, for example, we might compare vastly different diagnostic and treatment systems. These insights sensitively balance the poles of universalism and relativism. They also trouble the hegemonic view of mental illness as a biological disease based in neural circuits, and help us find a way through the universalism of global psychiatry to the social causes of mental disorder—and to link both elements.

Specifically, the book uncovered some epistemic shifts from culturalist and biological explanations of mental disorder, to an emphasis on "universal suffering," to the intertwining of chronic illness and chronic poverty, war, and the global marketization of pharmaceuticals. It approached mental disorder as a lens for analyzing forms of life, life–death struggles, and modes of recovery and dying. This is reflected in our methods, which have shifted from an emphasis on ethnography as an observational method, to a textual concern with writing and representation, through to current concerns with ethnography as a way to address existential questions about ourselves and others.

Perhaps anthropology's most valuable contribution is as a counterpoint to the reductive models of individual psychology, behavioral economics, and cultural and biological essentialism. Anthropology recognizes things are not always what they seem in the gap between concept and experience and reminds us that interpretation may be dangerous. Veena Das and various colleagues of hers have been influential in this endeavor. In her book *Affliction* (2015), Das argues there are "no well-made ontologies that could explain the movement of disease as it inhabits human bodies versus when it exists as an abstraction in textbooks or other discursive forms" (22). While illness narratives may force us to listen to patients and doctors, they also represent very formulaic notions of experience—as does the "fantasy" of statistics mapping the global burden of mental illness (17). Rather, Das proposes that we examine "how the experience of illness creates incoherence," and that we retain anthropology as a particular form of attentiveness to the fragile realities in which the fictionalization of illness and affliction occur, all the while staying open to other disciplines (17). Madness, she argues, may reveal the everyday contours of "normality," but it also tells us something about the "fragility of relations and of experience that is revealed when madness cannot be absorbed into the everyday" (84). Das sees diagnosis as an uncertain space where knowledge, treatment, and intervention enter, and which medics and caregivers must negotiate according to their capabilities and circumstances—and in doing so, she reminds us of Good's argument that diagnosis is a "dialogical moment" (88).

This book also gave central importance to varied relations of suffering and language, particularly to languages of representation, classification, and discourse. It highlighted many sophisticated arguments about the language of mental disorder. However, many terms that anthropologists use need greater precision. What exactly do "culture," "biology," "structure," and "interaction" mean? Precisely how does epigenetics differ from the "biosocial"? How do "bio-ethnographic" methods relate to these distinctions? How, for example, can new neuroscientific technologies aid treatments of mental disorder? And does global mental health activism mean emphasizing the conditions of world geography and power, or everyday life in local communities? Going forward, researchers will need to clarify these distinctions without losing the subtlety and detail that make our critiques valuable.

Criticizing the linguistic fallacies of definition is all very well. This book also emphasized the importance of moving away from abstract theory and pure intellectual critique to influence policy and people's actual needs (e.g., Wilkinson and Kleinman 2016). This needs careful thinking through. In a climate where scholarship is increasingly measured by its utility and "impact," our interventions increasingly demonstrate the discipline's contemporary relevance. This book cited many ways "making a difference" does not mean losing careful theorizing. Even philosophically informed anthropological theory can coexist with practical interventions. While Das's (2015) work, for example, is very philosophical, she has also conducted extensive household surveys over many years among Delhi neighborhoods to establish mortality rates and assisted health economists and policy makers working to profile and improve health in low-income settings.

Perhaps "insider–outsider" divides are not as unbridgeable as they may be imagined. Anthropologists have demonstrably assisted the development of culturally sensitive diagnoses and influenced the efficacy of medical, community, and therapeutic interventions. Jim Yong Kim, who was appointed president of the World Bank in 2012, is a medical anthropologist. Therefore, let us return to Good's (2012a) argument for "intervention as mode of inquiry." Good argues we should not use criticisms of the humanitarian industry and of the language of psychiatric classification as an excuse not to assist people affected by violence. Indeed, alongside his sophisticated theoretical work, Good has accompanied Institute of Medicine (IOM) mobile mental health teams and documented and evaluated civilian trauma and military violence while assisting mental health interventions in post-tsunami, post-conflict Indonesia (see also DelVecchio, Good, and Good 2013). Rather, he argues that clever theory should not eclipse or disdain intervention; these activities are and should be mutually dependent and reinforcing. He writes,

> We have been in a position to ask people to talk about their recovery
> precisely because we are involved in the intervention and its
> evaluation.... I would argue that we should not privilege intervention
> as the only ethical position from which to investigate and write about
> these issues, but that we should recognize involvement in intervention
> as one critical site for anthropological inquiry. Many things have
> become evident to us precisely because we have been trying to build
> systems of care—not only about the inner lives of those treated in the
> project, but also about the structure of health services and the difficulty
> of initiating change. (531)

We have seen how shifting borders between disciplines offer possibilities for exciting forms of dialogue. The anthropology of mental disorder is rapidly growing and changing. Inevitably, many debates are still normative. Are we, for example, concerned with "psycho-anthropology," psychological or psychiatric anthropology, "anthro-psychoanalysis," or an evolving something else? Are we researchers, observers, activists, therapists, or policy makers? Can the psychoanalytic session stand as a form of ethnography? Returning to Luhrmann's American study *Of Two Minds* (2001), certainly she could not have predicted the enormous extent to which biopsychiatry would eclipse psychoanalysis. Nor, perhaps, the serious ethnographic attention anthropologists would give the task of investigating fields of interior suffering usually reserved for psychoanalysis. Even so, we cannot privilege the unconscious over social and other reasons for "disordered" states and experience (Good 2012b). This would reproduce the colonial anthropology of "knowing better" than our subjects (Good 2012a: 526). We should also be mindful of claiming the expert position. Foucault's idea that the doctor-patient relationship is the site of authorial knowledge is difficult to sustain in a world where medicine and mental health are increasingly "democratized" (Dumit 2012), and in the hands of ordinary people who have no shortage of access to information and knowledge. Our problem, therefore, is not a lack of knowledge but of deciding which kinds of knowledge are useful, when, where, and for whom.

Anthropology allows us to move ethnographically between interior and social worlds. This book shows how subjectivity can and *should* go beyond inscribing the individual within categorical oppositions (or oppressions) of trauma and resilience, madness and sanity, health and illness, East and West, North and South. Analyzing subjectivity should arguably lead us to explore mental disorder ethnographically more deeply as a form of life itself (see Biehl, Good, and Kleinman 2007). This will require more than a single unified theory or mode of inquiry (Good 2012a: 531).

Finally, Lévi-Strauss likened the anthropologist to the schizophrenic who feels both insignificant and overimportant in society. In his essay "Cosmopolitanism and Schizophrenia," he portrayed the choice to be an anthropologist as one of living "forever dead to the world," in a condition of "chronic uprootedness" and a "psychologically mutilated" condition by virtue of the constant attempt to uncover humanity in all its expressions (quoted in Seigel 1994: 365). To subject oneself to the grief and suffering involved in undertaking work on mental disorder is certainly not easy. As Arthur Kleinman reflects in his essay "How We Endure" (2014),

> Patients endure greatly debilitating and painful disorders and some of the most trying therapeutic interventions with the hope of getting better. But many don't.... And we need, on occasion, to step outside ourselves and look in as if an observer on our endeavors and our relationships—personal and professional—to acknowledge the strength, compassion, courage, and humanity with which we ourselves endure or help to make bearable the hard journeys of others. These are the qualities that make acceptance and striving, if not noble, then certainly deeply human—worthy of respect of ourselves and those whose journeys we share. (119–20)

To conclude, anthropologists have shown us that when deep perceptions of life and endurance become embedded into their theories, they lay the ground for a rich ethics of engagement and advocacy. If we begin in the classroom, we will hopefully be better equipped to enter the world of professionals and practitioners. This book takes one step toward working through some difficult questions we have posed for ourselves. This work needs to continue. Thus, we must continue to explore questions such as: How does a diagnosis find, free, constrain, and define people? What use are sophisticated writings about suffering if they do not improve people's lives? How do we envisage our knowledge in the hands of mental health professionals? How do people want to repair their own worlds compared with experts who speak on their behalf? What differences characterize anthropologists working in global mental health versus cultural and community psychiatry? What kinds of certainty arise from our work, our loud claims, and hesitant whispers—how and why?

APPENDIX I: RECOMMENDED RESOURCES

Indicative Journals

Indicative Journals   **101**

American Anthropologist
American Ethnologist
Anthropology & Medicine
Cultural Anthropology
Culture, Medicine and Psychiatry
Culture and Psychology
Ethnos
Ethos
Hau: Journal of Ethnographic Theory
Indian Journal of Psychiatry
Journal of the Royal Anthropological Institute
Medical Anthropology
Medical Anthropology Quarterly
Medical Humanities
Philosophy, Ethics and Humanities in Medicine
Philosophy, Psychiatry and Psychology
Science as Culture. Science in Context
Social Science & Medicine
Theory, Culture and Society
Theory and Psychology
Transcultural Psychiatry
Visual Anthropology Review

Selected Online Visual Anthropology Resources

Psycho Cultural Cinema http://psychoculturalcinema.com/author/
    lemelson/
Royal Anthropological Institute Film Library http://www.therai.org.uk/
    film/film.html
Society for Visual Anthropology http://societyforvisualanthropology.org/
Visual Anthropology http://www.visualanthropology.net/
Visual Ethnography http://www.vejournal.org/index.php/vejournal/
    index

Selected Website and Blog Resources

H-Madness http://historypsychiatry.com/
Medical Humanities http://medhum.med.nyu.edu/blog/
Mind Hacks http://mindhacks.com/
Neuroanthropology http://blogs.plos.org/neuroanthropology/
Savage Minds http://savageminds.org/
Somatosphere: Science, Medicine, and Anthropology http://somatosphere.
    net/resources
102   The Foundation for Psychocultural Research- http://www.thefpr.org/

REFERENCES

Abraham, Henry D. 2014. "When the Trip Doesn't End." *Psychologist* 27: 670–73.

Abu-Lughod, Lila. 2002. "Do Muslim Women Really Need Saving? Anthropological Reflections on Cultural Relativism and Its Others." *American Anthropologist* 104 (3): 783–90. http://dx.doi.org/10.1525/aa.2002.104.3.783.

Abu-Lughod, Lila. 1991. "Writing against Culture." In *Recapturing Anthropology: Working in the Present*, edited by Richard Fox, 137–62. Santa Fe: School of American Research Press.

Aggarwal, Neil, Ravi Desilva, Andel V. Nicasio, Marit Boiler, and Roberto Lewis-Fernández. 2015. "Does the Cultural Formulation Interview for the Fifth Revision of the Diagnostic and Statistical Manual of Mental Disorders (DSM-5) Affect Medical Communication? A Qualitative Exploratory Study from the New York Site." *Ethnicity & Health* 20 (1): 1–28. http://dx.doi.org/10.1080/13557858.2013.857762.

Aggarwal, Neil Krishan, Peter Lam, Enrico Castillo, Mitchell Weiss, Esperanza Diaz, Renato Alarcön, Rob Van Dijk, et al. 2015. "How Do Clinicians Prefer Cultural Competence Training? Findings from the DSM-5 Cultural Formulation Interview Field Trial." *Academic Psychiatry*, 8 October, online publication. http://dx.doi.org/10.1007/s40596-015-0429-3.

Aggarwal, Neil K., Andel V. Nicasio, Ravi DeSilva, Marit Boiler, and Roberto Lewis-Fernández. 2013. "Barriers to Implementing the DSM-5 Cultural Formulation Interview: A Qualitative Study." *Culture, Medicine and Psychiatry* 37 (3): 505–33. http://dx.doi.org/10.1007/s11013-013-9325-z.

Amaro, Hortensia, Mary Jo Larson, Joanne Gampel, Erin Richardson, Andrea Savage, and Debra Wagler. 2005. "Racial/Ethnic Differences in Social Vulnerability among Women with Co-occurring Mental Health and Substance Abuse Disorders." *Journal of Community Psychology* 33 (4): 495–511. http://dx.doi.org/10.1002/jcop.20065.

American Psychiatric Association (APA). 2013. *Diagnostic and Statistical Manual of Mental Disorders, Fifth Edition* (DSM-5). Arlington, VA: APA.

American Psychiatric Association (APA). 1994. *Diagnostic and Statistical Manual of Mental Disorders, Fourth Edition* (DSM-IV). Arlington, VA: APA.

American Psychiatric Association (APA). 1980. *Diagnostic and Statistical Manual of Mental Disorders, Third Edition* (DSM-III). Arlington, VA: APA.

Anderson, C. Broughton. 2010. "Fassin, Didier and Richard Rechtman. 2009. The Empire of Trauma: An Inquiry into the Condition of Victimhood. Princeton, New Jersey: Princeton University Press." *Anthropological Notebooks* 16 (1): 107–08.

Anderson-Fye, Eileen, and Jerry Floersch. 2011. "'I'm Not Your Typical "Homework Stresses Me Out" Kind of Girl': Psychological Anthropology in Research on College Student Usage of Psychiatric Medications and Mental Health Services." *Ethos* 39 (4): 501–21. http://dx.doi.org/10.1111/j.1548-1352.2011.01209.x.

Angst, Jules. 1966. "On the Etiology and Nosology of Endogenous Depressive Psychoses: A Genetic, Sociologic and Clinical Study" (in German). *Monographien aus dem Gesamtgebiete der Neurologie und Psychiatrie* 112: 1–118.

Appignanesi, Lisa. 2008. *Mad, Bad and Sad: A History of Women and Mind Doctors from 1800*. London: Virago.

Apthorpe, Raymond. 2014. "Anthropology and Humanitarianisms across Borders: A Growing Field of Study." *Journal of the Royal Anthropological Institute* 20 (2): 357–61. http://dx.doi.org/10.1111/1467-9655.12108.

Asad, Talal. 2011. "Thinking about the Secular Body, Pain and Liberal Politics." *Cultural Anthropology* 26 (4): 657–75.

Baer, Roberta, Lauren Clark, and Caroline Peterson. 1998. "Folk Illnesses." In *Handbook of Immigrant Health*, edited by Sana Loue, 183–202. New York: Plenum. http://dx.doi.org/10.1007/978-1-4899-1936-6_10.

Bakhtin, Mikhail. 1986. *Speech Genres and Other Late Essays*. Translated by Vern McGee. Austin: University of Texas Press.

Basilico, Matthew, Jonathon Weigel, Anjali Motgi, Jacob Bor, and Salmaan Keshavjee. 2013. "Health for All? Competing Theories and Geopolitics." In *Reimagining Global Health*, edited by Paul Farmer, Jim Yong Kim, Arthur Kleinman, and Matthew Basilico, 74–110. Berkeley: University of California Press.

Bateson, Gregory. 1972. *Collected Essays in Anthropology, Psychiatry, Evolution, and Epistemology*. Chicago: University of Chicago Press.

Bateson, Gregory, Don D. Jackson, Jay Haley, and John Weakland. 1956. "Toward a Theory of Schizophrenia." *Behavioral Science* 1 (4): 251–54.

Becker, Anne, Anjali Motji, Jonathon Weigel, Giuseppe Raviola, Salmaan Keshavjee, and Arthur Kleinman. 2013. "The Unique Challenges of Mental Health and MDRTB: Critical Perspectives on Metrics of Disease." In *Reimagining Global Health*, edited by Paul Farmer, Jim Yong Kim, Arthur Kleinman, and Matthew Basilico, 212–44. Berkeley: University of California Press.

Bell, Vaughan. 2014. "Cultures of Chemically-Induced Hallucinations." *Psychologist* 27: 666–69.

Bemme, Doerte, and Nicole D'Souza. 2014. "Global Mental Health and Its Discontents: An Inquiry into the Making of Global and Local Scale." *Transcultural Psychiatry* 51 (6): 850–74. http://dx.doi.org/10.1177/1363461514539830.

Bemme, Doerte, and Nicole D'Souza. 2012. Global Mental Health and Its Discontents. Somatosphere. Available at: http://somatosphere.net/2012/07/global-mental-health-and-its-discontents.html (accessed 6 November 2014).

Benedict, Ruth. 1934a. "Anthropology and the Abnormal." In *An Anthropologist at Work: Writings of Ruth Benedict*, edited by Margaret Mead, 262–83. New York: Avon Books.

Benedict, Ruth. [1934b] 2005. *Patterns of Culture*. New York: Houghton Mifflin Harcourt.

Benjamin, Walter. 1969. "Illuminations." In *Theses on the Philosophy of History*, edited by Hannah Arendt, 83–109. New York: Schocken.

Biehl, João. 2005. *Vita: Life in a Zone of Social Abandonment*. Berkeley: University of California Press.

Biehl, João, Byron Good, and Arthur Kleinman. 2007. *Subjectivity: Ethnographic Investigations*. Berkeley: University of California Press. http://dx.doi.org/10.1525/california/9780520247925.001.0001.

Bleuler, Eugen. [1911] 1950. *Dementia Praecox or the Group of Schizophrenias*. New York: International Universities Press.

Bollas, Christopher. 2002. *Free Association*. Birmingham, UK: Ikon Books.

Bolton, Gillie, Stephanie Howlett, Colin Lago, and Jeannie Wright, eds. 2004. *Writing Cures: An Introductory Handbook of Writing in Counselling and Therapy*. London: Brunner/ Routledge.

Borneman, John. 2011. "Daydreaming, Intimacy, and the Intersubjective Third in Fieldwork Encounters in Syria." *American Ethnologist* 38 (2): 234–48. http://dx.doi.org/10.1111/j.1548-1425.2011.01303.x.

Boyle, Mary. 2004. "Schizophrenia and Genetics: Does Critical Thought Stop Here?" *Journal of Critical Psychology, Counselling and Psychotherapy* 4: 78–85.

Boyle, Mary. 2002. *Schizophrenia: A Scientific Delusion*. 2nd ed. London: Routledge.

Brewin, Chris, Ruth Lanius, Andrei Novac, Ulrich Schnyder, and Sandro Galea. 2009. "Reformulating PTSD for DSM-V: Life after Criterion A." *Journal of Traumatic Stress* 22 (5): 366–73. http://dx.doi.org/10.1002/jts.20443.

Brodwin, Paul. 2013. *Everyday Ethics: Voices from the Front Line of Community Psychiatry*. Berkeley: University of California Press.

Brown, George W., and Tirril Harris, eds. 1978. *Social Origins of Depression: A Study of Psychiatric Disorder in Women*. London: Tavistock.

Burton, Robert. [1621] 2001. *The Anatomy of Melancholy*. New York: New York Review of Books.

Burton-Bradley, G.B. 1985. "The Amok Syndrome in Papua and New Guinea." In *The Culture-Bound Syndromes: Folk Illnesses of Psychiatric and Anthropological Interest*, edited by Ronald Simons and Charles C. Hughes, 237–50. Dordrecht, Holland: Reidel Publishing. http://dx.doi.org/10.1007/978-94-009-5251-5_22.

Canguilhem, Georges. [1966] 1991. *The Normal and the Pathological*. Rev. ed. Introduction by Michel Foucault. Translated by Carolyn R. Fawcett. New York: Zone Books. First published as *Le Normale et le Pathologique*. Paris: Presses Universitaire de France.

Carhart-Harris, Robin, Mendel Kaelen, and David Nutt. 2014. "How Do Hallucinogens Work on the Brain?" *Psychologist* 27: 662–65.

Carothers, John C. 1951. "Frontal Lobe Function and the African." *Journal of Mental Science* 97: 12–48.

Cavell, Stanley. 1996. "Comments on Veena Das' Essay 'Language and Body: Transactions in the Construction of Pain.'" *Daedalus* 125: 93–98.

Chowdhary, Neerja, Arpita Anand, Sona Dimidjian, Sachin Shinde, Benedict Weobong, Madhumitha Balaji, Steven D. Hollon, et al. 2016. "The Healthy Activity Program Lay Counsellor Delivered Treatment for Severe Depression in India: Systematic Development and Randomised Evaluation." *British Journal of Psychiatry* 208 (4): 381–88. http://dx.doi.org/10.1192/bjp.bp.114.161075.

Clark, Jocalyn. 2014. "Medicalization of Global Health 2: The Medicalization of Global Mental Health." *Global Health Action* 7 (10): 1–6.

Clifford, James, and George Marcus, eds. 1986. *Writing Culture: The Poetics and Politics of Ethnography*. Berkeley: University of California Press.

Collins, Pamela, Vikram Patel, Sarah Joestl, Dana March, Thomas Insel, Abdallah Daar, Isabel A. Bordin, et al. 2011. "Grand Challenges in Global Mental Health." *Nature* 475 (7354): 27–30. http://dx.doi.org/10.1038/475027a.

Corin, Ellen. 2014. "The Work of the Other." *Clio's Psyche* 29: S456–60.

Corin, Ellen, and Gilles Lauzon. 1992. "Positive Withdrawal and the Quest for Meaning: The Reconstruction of Experience among Schizophrenics." *Psychiatry* 55: 266–78.

Costandi, Moheb. 2014. "Looking Back: A Brief History of Psychedelic Psychiatry." *Psychologist* 27: 714–5.

Crapanzano, Vincent. 2006. "The Scene: Shadowing the Real." *Anthropological Theory* 6 (4): 387–405. http://dx.doi.org/10.1177/1463499606071593.

Crapanzano, Vincent. 1985. *Tuhami: Portrait of a Moroccan*. Chicago: University of Chicago Press.

Csordas, Thomas. 2007. "Book Review of João Biehl, *Vita: Life in a Zone of Social Abandonment*." *American Ethnologist* 34: 2009–12. http://dx.doi.org/10.1525/ae.2007.34.2.2009.

Cummings, Constance. 2013. DSM-5 on Culture: A Significant Advance. The fpr.org blog. Available at: http://thefprorg.wordpress.com/2013/06/27/dsm-5-on-culture-a-significant-advance/ (accessed 7 February 2014).

Daniel, E. Valentine. 1996. "Crushed Glass, or, Is There a Counterpoint to Culture?" In *Culture/Contexture: Explorations in Anthropology and Literary Studies*, edited by E. V. Daniel and J. M. Peek, 357–75. Berkeley: University of California Press.

Das, Anindya. 2011. "Farmers' Suicide in India: Implications for Public Mental Health." *International Journal of Social Psychiatry* 57 (1): 21–29.

Das, Anindya, and Mohan Rao. 2012. "Universal Mental Health: Re-Evaluating the Call for Global Mental Health." *Critical Public Health* 22 (4): 383–89. http://dx.doi.org/10.1080/09581596.2012.700393.

Das, Veena. 2015. *Affliction: Health, Disease, Poverty*. New York: Fordham University Press. http://dx.doi.org/10.5422/fordham/9780823261802.001.0001.

Das, Veena. 2010. "Book Review of *The Empire of Trauma: An Inquiry into the Condition of Victimhood*, by Didier Fassin and Richard Rechtman. Translated by Rachel Gomme." *American Journal of Sociology* 116 (2): 676–78. http://dx.doi.org/10.1086/655950.

Das, Veena. 2007a. *Life and Words*. Berkeley: University of California Press.

Das, Veena. 2007b. "Commentary: Trauma and Testimony, between Law and Discipline." *Ethos* 35 (3): 330–35. http://dx.doi.org/10.1525/eth.2007.35.3.330.

Das, Veena. 1996. "Language and Body: Transactions in the Construction of Pain." *Daedalus* 125: 67–91.

Daudet, Alphonse. 2002. *In the Land of Pain*. Translated by Julian Barnes. London: Jonathon Cape.

Davis, Elizabeth Anne. 2012. *Bad Souls: Madness and Responsibility in Modern Greece*. Durham, NC: Duke University Press.

Dein, Simon. 2013. "Religion and Mental Health: The Contribution of Anthropology." *World Psychiatry* 12 (1): 34–35. http://dx.doi.org/10.1002/wps.20007.

Dein, Simon. 2010. "Judeo-Christian Religious Experience and Psychopathology: The Legacy of William James." *Transcultural Psychiatry* 47 (4): 523–47. http://dx.doi. org/10.1177/1363461510377568.

Dein, Simon, Christopher Cook, and Harold Koenig. 2012. "Religion, Spirituality, and Mental Health: Current Controversies and Future Directions." *Journal of Nervous and Mental Disease* 200 (10): 852–55. http://dx.doi.org/10.1097/ NMD.ob013e31826b6dle.

Dein, Simon, and Roland Littlewood. 2011. "Religion and Psychosis: A Common Evolutionary Trajectory?" *Transcultural Psychiatry* 48 (3): 318–35. http://dx.doi. org/10.1177/1363461511402723.

Dein, Simon, and Roland Littlewood. 2007. "The Voice of God." *Anthropology & Medicine* 14 (2): 213–28. http://dx.doi.org/10.1080/13648470701381515.

De Lauri, Antonio, ed. 2016. *The Politics of Humanitarianism: Power, Ideology and Aid.* London: I. B. Tauris.

DelVecchio Good, Mary-Jo, and Byron Good. 2013. "Perspectives on the Politics of Peace in Aceh, Indonesia." In *Radical Egalitarianism: Local Realities, Global Relations,* edited by Felicity Aulino, Miriam Goheen, and Stanley Tambiah, 191–208. New York: Fordham University Press.

DelVecchio Good, Mary-Jo, Sarah Teresa Hyde, Sarah Pinto, and Byron Good, eds. 2008. *Postcolonial Disorders.* Berkeley: University of California Press.

Denham, Aaron. 2014. "Psychoanalytic Anthropology." *Clio's Psyche* 29: 383–94.

Descola, Philippe. 2013. *Beyond Nature and Culture.* Chicago: University of Chicago Press.

Desjarlais, Robert. 1989. "Healing through Images: The Magical Flight and Healing Geography of Nepali Shamanism." *Ethos* 17 (3): 289–307. http://dx.doi.org/10.1525/ eth.1989.17.3.02a00020.

Devereux, George. 1980. *Basic Problems of Ethnopsychiatry.* Translated by Basia Miller Gulati and George Devereux. Chicago: University of Chicago Press.

Dick, Lyle. 2002. "Aboriginal-European Relations during the Great Age of North Polar Exploration." *Polar Geography* 26 (1): 66–86. http://dx.doi. org/10.1080/789609354.

Dick, Lyle. 1995. "'Pibloktoq' (Arctic Hysteria): A Construction of European-Inuit Relations?" *Arctic Anthropology* 32: 1–42.

Dow, James. 1986. "Universal Aspects of Symbolic Healing: A Theoretical Synthesis." *American Anthropologist* 88 (1): 56–69. http://dx.doi.org/10.1525/ aa.1986.88.1.02a00040.

Dressler, William. 2012. "Cultural Consonance: Linking Culture, the Individual and Health." *Preventive Medicine* 55 (5): 390–93. http://dx.doi.org/10.1016/j.ypmed.2011.12.022.

Dumit, Joseph. 2012. *Drugs for Life: How Pharmaceutical Companies Define Our Health.* Durham, NC: Duke University Press. http://dx.doi.org/10.1215/9780822393481.

Dura-Vila, Gloria, Simon Dein, Roland Littlewood, and Gerard Leavey. 2010. "The Dark Night of the Soul: Causes and Resolution of Emotional Distress among Contemplative Nuns." *Transcultural Psychiatry* 47 (4): 548–70. http://dx.doi. org/10.1177/1363461510374899.

Edgar, Robert, and Hilary Sapire. 2000. *African Apocalypse: The Story of Nontetha Nkwenkwe, a Twentieth-Century South African Prophet.* Johannesburg: Witwatersrand University Press.

Edwards, James. 1985. "Indigenous *Koro*: A Genital Retraction Syndrome of Insular South-East Asia: A Critical Review." In *The Culture-Bound Syndromes. Folk Illnesses of Psychiatric and Anthropological Interest*, edited by Ronald Simons and Charles C. Hughes, 169–91. Dordrecht, Holland: Reidel Publishing. http://dx.doi.org/10.1007/978-94-009-5251-5_17.

Estroff, Sue. 1981. *Making It Crazy.* Berkeley: University of California Press.

Fanon, Frantz. [1963] 2001. "Colonial War and Mental Disorder." In *The Wretched of the Earth.* Translated by Constance Farrington, 200–50. London: Penguin.

Farmer, Paul. 2005. *Pathologies of Power.* Berkeley: University of California Press.

Farmer, Paul, Jim Yong Kim, Arthur Kleinman, and Matthew Basilico, eds. 2013. *Reimagining Global Health.* Berkeley: University of California Press.

Fassin, Didier. 2011. *A Critique of Humanitarian Reason: A Moral History of the Present.* Princeton, NJ: Princeton University Press. http://dx.doi.org/10.1525/california/9780520271166.001.0001.

Fassin, Didier. 2007. "Humanitarianism as a Politics of Life." *Public Culture* 19 (3): 499–520.

Fassin, Didier, and Richard Rechtman. 2009. *The Empire of Trauma: An Inquiry into the Condition of Victimhood.* Translated by Rachel Gomme. Princeton, NJ: Princeton University Press.

Fernando, Suman. 2014. *Mental Health World Wide: Culture, Globalization and Development.* Basingstoke, UK: Palgrave Macmillan.

Fernando, Suman. 2010. "A 'Global' Mental Health Program or Markets for Big Pharma?" *Open Mind* (September & October). http://www.sumanfernando.com/Global%20Program%20&%20Big%20Pharma.pdf.

Fonseca, Claudia. 2006. "Book Review of Biehl, João, *Vita: Life in a Zone of Social Abandonment.*" *Journal of the Royal Anthropological Institute* 12: 686–87. http://dx.doi.org/10.1111/j.1467-9655.2006.00359_11.x.

Foucault, Michel. 2006. *History of Madness.* Edited by Jean Khalfa. Translated by Jonathon Murphy and Jean Khalfa. London: Routledge.

Foucault, Michel. 1965. *Madness and Civilization: A History of Insanity in the Age of Reason.* Translated by Richard Howard. London: Tavistock.

Frank, Jerome D., and Julia Frank. 1991. *Persuasion and Healing. A Comparative Study of Psychotherapy.* Baltimore: Johns Hopkins University Press.

Freedman, Robert. 2009. *The Madness within Us: Schizophrenia as a Neuronal Process.* New York: Oxford University Press.

Freud, Sigmund. [1917] 2005. "Mourning and Melancholia." In *On Murder, Mourning and Melancholia.* Translated by Shaun Whiteside, 201–19. London: Penguin.

Freud, Sigmund. [1920] 2003. *Beyond the Pleasure Principle.* Translated by John Reddick. London: Penguin.

Freud, Sigmund. [1894] 1966. *The Neuropsychoses of Defence.* Translated by James Strachey. London: Hogarth Press.

REFERENCES

Galton, Francis. 1869. *Hereditary Genius*. London: Macmillan and Co. http://dx.doi. org/10.1037/13474-000.

Garcia, Angela. 2010. *The Pastoral Clinic: Addiction and Dispossession along the Rio Grande*. Berkeley: University of California Press.

Garcia, Angela. 2008. "The Elegiac Addict: History, Chronicity, and the Melancholic Subject." *Cultural Anthropology* 23 (4): 718–46. http://dx.doi. org/10.1111/j.1548-1360.2008.00024.x.

Gee, Joanna, and Del Loewenthal. 2011. "Working with Despair: A Phenomenological Investigation." *Psychology and Psychotherapy: Theory, Research and Practice*. http:// dx.doi.org/10.1111/j.2044-8341.2011.02053.x.

Geertz, Clifford. 1988. *Works and Lives: The Anthropologist as Author*. Stanford, CA: Stanford University Press.

Geertz, Clifford. 1977. *The Interpretation of Cultures*. New York: Basic Books.

Goddard, Michael. 2011. *Out of Place: Madness in the Highlands of Papua New Guinea*. New York: Berghahn Books.

Gone, Joseph. 2014. "Colonial Genocide and Historical Trauma in Native North America: Complicating Contemporary Attributions." In *Colonial Genocide and Indigenous North America*, edited by Andrew Woolford, Jeff Benvenuto, and Alexander Hinton, 273–91. Durham, NC: Duke University Press. http://dx.doi. org/10.1215/9780822376149-013.

Gone, Joseph. 2013. "Redressing First Nations Historical Trauma: Theorizing Mechanisms for Indigenous Culture as Mental Health Treatment." *Transcultural Psychiatry* 50 (5): 683–706. http://dx.doi.org/10.1177/1363461513487669.

Good, Byron. 2012a. "Theorizing the 'Subject' of Medical and Psychiatric Anthropology." *Journal of the Royal Anthropological Institute* 18 (3): 515–35. http:// dx.doi.org/10.1111/j.1467-9655.2012.01774.x.

Good, Byron. 2012b. "Phenomenology, Psychoanalysis and Subjectivity in Java." *Ethos* 40 (1): 24–36. http://dx.doi.org/10.1111/j.1548-1352.2011.01229.x.

Good, Byron. 1994. *Medicine, Rationality and Experience. An Anthropological Perspective*. Cambridge: Cambridge University Press.

Good, Byron, Carla Manchira, Nida Ul Hasnat, Muhana Sofiati, and Utami Subandi. 2010. "Is 'Chronicity' Inevitable for Psychotic Illness? Studying Heterogeneity in the Course of Schizophrenia in Yogyakarta, Indonesia." In *Chronic Conditions, Fluid States: Chronicity and the Anthropology of Illness*, edited by Lenore Manderson and Carolyn Smith-Morris, 544–72. New Brunswick, NJ: Rutgers University Press.

Greenberg, David, Moshe Kalian, and Eliezer Witztum. 2010. "Value-Sensitive Psychiatric Rehabilitation." *Transcultural Psychiatry* 47 (4): 629–46. http://dx.doi. org/10.1177/1363461510383745.

Greene, Jeremy, Marguerite Thorp Basilico, Heidi Kim, and Paul Farmer. 2013. "Colonial Medicine and Its Legacies." In *Reimagining Global Health*, edited by Paul Farmer, Jim Yong Kim, Arthur Kleinman, and Matthew Basilico, 33–73. Berkeley: University of California Press.

Guarnaccia, Peter, Glorisa Canino, Maritza Rubio-Stipec, and Milagros Bravo. 1993. "The Prevalence of *Ataques de Nervios* in the Puerto Rico Disaster Study." *Journal of Nervous and Mental Disease* 181 (3): 157–65. http://dx.doi. org/10.1097/00005053-199303000-00003.

Guarnaccia, Peter, Igda Martinez, Rafael Ramirez, and Glorisa Canino. 2005. "Are *Ataques de Nervios* in Puerto Rican Children Associated with Psychiatric Disorder?" *Journal of the American Academy of Child and Adolescent Psychiatry* 44 (11): 1184–92. http://dx.doi.org/10.1097/01.chi.0000177059.34031.5d.

Guarnaccia, Peter J., Roberto Lewis-Fernández, Igda Martinez Pincay, Patrick Shrout, Jing Guo, Maria Torres, Glorisa Canino, and Margarita Alegria. 2010. "*Ataque de Nervios* as a Marker of Social and Psychiatric Vulnerability: Results from the NLAAS." *International Journal of Social Psychiatry* 56 (3): 298–309. http://dx.doi.org/10.1177/0020764008101636.

Guarnaccia, Peter J., and Lloyd H. Rogler. 1999. "Research on Culture-Bound Syndromes: New Directions." *American Journal of Psychiatry* 156 (9): 1322–27.

Gunnell, David, and Michael Eddleston. 2003. "Suicide by Intentional Ingestion of Pesticides: A Continuing Tragedy in Developing Countries." *International Journal of Epidemiology* 32 (6): 902–09. http://dx.doi.org/10.1093/ije/dyg307.

Gureje, Oye, Gregory Simon, Tevfik Ustun, and David P. Goldberg. 1997. "Somatization in Cross-Cultural Perspective: A World Health Organization Study in Primary Care." *American Journal of Psychiatry* 154 (7): 989–95. http://dx.doi.org/10.1176/ajp.154.7.989.

Hacking, Ian. 2002. *Mad Travelers: Reflections on the Reality of Transient Mental Illnesses*. Cambridge, MA: Harvard University Press.

Hacking, Ian. 1999. "Madness: Biological or Constructed?" In *The Social Construction of What?* edited by Ian Hacking, 100–24. Cambridge, MA: Harvard University Press.

Halliburton, Murphy. 2004. "Finding a Fit: Psychiatric Pluralism in South India and Its Implications for WHO Studies of Mental Disorder." *Transcultural Psychiatry* 41 (1): 80–98.

Han, Clara. 2012. *Life in Debt: Times of Care and Violence in Neoliberal Chile*. Berkeley: University of California Press.

Hansen, Thomas Blom. 2012. *Melancholia of Freedom: Social Life in an Indian Township in South Africa*. Princeton, NJ: Princeton University Press.

Harvey, David. 2000. *Spaces of Hope*. Berkeley: University of California Press.

Healy, David, Derelie Mangin, and David Antonuccio. 2013. "Data Based Medicine and Clinical Judgement." *International Journal of Risk and Safety in Medicine* 25 (2): 111–21.

Herman, Judith. 1992. *Trauma and Recovery*. New York: Basic Books.

Hinton, Devon, and Byron Good, eds. 2009. *Culture and Panic Disorder*. Stanford, CA: Stanford University Press.

Hinton, Devon, and Laurence Kirmayer. 2013. "Local Responses to Trauma: Symptom, Affect, and Healing." *Transcultural Psychiatry* 50 (5): 607–21. http://dx.doi.org/10.1177/1363461513506529.

Hinton, Devon, and Roberto Lewis-Fernández. 2011. "The Cross-Cultural Validity of Posttraumatic Stress Disorder: Implications for DSM-5." *Depression and Anxiety* 28 (9): 783–801. http://dx.doi.org/10.1002/da.20753.

Hollan, Douglas. 2013. "Coping in Plain Sight: Work as a Local Response to Event-Related Emotional Distress in Contemporary US Society." *Transcultural Psychiatry* 50 (5): 726–43. http://dx.doi.org/10.1177/1363461513488077.

Hopper, Kim. 2007. "Rethinking Social Recovery in Schizophrenia: What a Capabilities Approach Might Offer." *Social Science & Medicine* 65 (5): 868–79. http://dx.doi.org/10.1016/j.socscimed.2007.04.012.

Hopper, Kim. 2004. "Interrogating the Meaning of Culture in the WHO International Studies of Schizophrenia." In *Schizophrenia, Culture and Subjectivity*, edited by Janis Jenkins and Robert Barrett, 62–87. Cambridge: Cambridge University Press.

Hopper, Kim, Glynn Harrison, Aleksandar Janca, and Norman Sartorius. 2007. *Recovery from Schizophrenia: An International Perspective*. Oxford: Oxford University Press.

Horwitz, Allan V. 2002. *Creating Mental Illness*. Chicago: University of Chicago Press.

Horwitz, Allan, and Jerome Wakefield. 2007. *The Loss of Sorrow*. Oxford: Oxford University Press.

Horowitz, Donald. 2002. *The Deadly Ethnic Riot*. Berkeley: University of California Press.

House, Richard, and Del Loewenthal. 2009. "Editorial Introduction: 'Therapeutic Ethos' in Therapeutic, Educational and Cultural Perspective." In *Childhood, Well-Being and a Therapeutic Ethos*, edited by Richard House and Del Loewenthal, 1–16. London: Karnac.

Ingelby, David. 2014. "Global Mental Health." In *Cultural Sociology of Mental Illness: An A–Z Guide*, edited by Andrew T. Scull, 334–35. Thousand Oaks, CA: Sage Publications.

Insel, Thomas. 2011. "Director's Blog: Mental Illness Defined as Disruption in Neural Circuits." National Institute of Mental Health, August 12. Available at: http://www.nimh.nih.gov/about/director/2011/mental-illness-defined-as-disruption-in-neural-circuits.shtml (accessed 9 September 2014).

Jablensky, Assen, and Norman Sartorius. 2008. "What Did the WHO Studies Really Find?" *Schizophrenia Bulletin* 34: 253–55.

James, Erica C. 2010. *Democratic Insecurities: Violence, Trauma, and Intervention in Haiti*. Berkeley: University of California Press.

Jamison, Kay. 2011. *An Unquiet Mind: A Memoir of Moods and Madness*. London: Picador.

Jenkins, Janis Hunter, and Robert Barratt, eds. 2004. *Schizophrenia, Culture and Subjectivity: The Edge of Experience*. Cambridge: Cambridge University Press.

Jones, Jim. 2011. *A Hidden Madness*. Louisiana: Quid Pro Quo.

Jones, Nev, and Timothy Kelly. 2015. "Inconvenient Complications: On the Heterogeneities of Madness and Their Relationship to Disability." In *Madness, Distress and the Politics of Disablement*, edited by Helen Spandler, Jill Anderson, and Bob Sapey, 43–56. Bristol, UK: Policy Press.

Kadison, Richard. 2005. "Getting an Edge—Use of Stimulants and Antidepressants in College." *New England Journal of Medicine* 353: 1089–91. http://dx.doi.org/10.1056/NEJMp058047.

Kahlbaum, Karl L. 1874. *Catatonia of Tension Madness. A Clinical Form of Psychical Illness*. Berlin: Hirschwald.

Kapferer, Bruce. 2013. "How Anthropologists Think: Configurations of the Exotic." *Journal of the Royal Anthropological Institute* 19 (4): 813–36. http://dx.doi.org/10.1111/1467-9655.12066.

Keller, Richard. 2007. *Colonial Madness. Psychiatry in French North Africa*. Chicago: University of Chicago Press. http://dx.doi.org/10.7208/chicago/9780226429779.001.0001.

Khan, Nichola. Forthcoming, 2016. "1994. Political Madness, Ethics and Story-Making in Liaquatabad District in Karachi." In *Cityscapes of Violence in Karachi: Publics and Counterpublics*, edited by Nichola Khan. London: Hurst Publishers.

Khan, Nichola. 2013a. "A Moving Heart: Querying a Singular Problem of 'Immobility' in Afghan Migration to the UK." *Medical Anthropology: Cross-Cultural Studies in Health and Illness* 32 (6): 518–34. http://dx.doi.org/10.1080/01459740.2012.757607.

Khan, Nichola. 2013b. "'From Refugees to the World Stage': Sport, Civilisation and Modernity in *Out of the Ashes* and the UK Afghan Diaspora." *South Asian Popular Culture* 11 (3): 271–85. http://dx.doi.org/10.1080/14746689.2013.820478.

Khan, Nichola. 2010. "Violence, Anti-/Convention and Desires for Transformation amongst Pakistan's Mohajirs in Karachi." *Cultural Dynamics* 22 (3): 225–45. http://dx.doi.org/10.1177/0921374010383854.

Kirmayer, Laurence. 2015. "Re-visioning Psychiatry: Toward an Ecology of Mind in Health and Illness." In *Re-Visioning Psychiatry. Cultural Phenomenology, Critical Neuroscience, and Global Mental Health*, edited by Laurence J. Kirmayer, Robert Lemelson, and Constance Cummings, 622–60. New York: Cambridge University Press. http://dx.doi.org/10.1017/CBO9781139424745.027.

Kirmayer, Laurence, J. 2013. "Cultural Psychiatry Lecture #1: Cultural Psychiatry: A Critical Introduction, Part 1." Available at: https://www.mcgill.ca/tcpsych/videos/courses/cultural-psychiatry#INTRODUCTION (accessed 21 June 2016).

Kirmayer, Laurence. 2007. "Psychotherapy and the Cultural Concept of the Person." *Transcultural Psychiatry* 44: 232–57.

Kirmayer, Laurence. 1993. "Healing and the Invention of Metaphor: the Effectiveness of Symbols Revisited." *Culture, Medicine and Psychiatry* 17 (2): 161–95. http://dx.doi.org/10.1007/BF01379325.

Kirmayer, Laurence. 1986. "Somatization and the Social Construction of Illness Experience." In *Illness Behavior: A Multidisciplinary Model*, edited by Sean McHugh, and T. Michael Vallis, 111–33. New York: Plenum. http://dx.doi.org/10.1007/978-1-4684-5257-0_7.

Kirmayer, Laurence. 1984. "Culture, Affect and Somatization: Part I." *Transcultural Psychiatry* 21 (3): 159–88. http://dx.doi.org/10.1177/136346158402100301.

Kirmayer, Laurence, and Lauren Ban. 2013. "Cultural Psychiatry: Research Strategies and Future Directions." *Advances in Psychosomatic Medicine* 33: 97–114. http://dx.doi.org/10.1159/000348742.

Kirmayer, Laurence, and Caminee Blake. 2009. "Theoretical Perspectives on the Cross-Cultural Study of Panic Disorder." In *Culture and Panic Disorder*, edited by Devon Hinton and Byron Good, 31–56. Stanford, CA: Stanford University Press.

Kirmayer, Laurence, Joseph Gone, and Joshua Moses. 2014. "Rethinking Historical Trauma." *Transcultural Psychiatry* 51 (3): 299–319. http://dx.doi.org/10.1177/1363461514536358.

Kirmayer, Laurence, Robert Lemelson, and Constance Cummings, eds. 2015. *Revisioning Psychiatry. Integrating Biological, Clinical and Cultural Perspectives*. Cambridge: Cambridge University Press.

Kirmayer, Laurence, and Joel Robbins, eds. 1991. *Current Concepts of Somatization: Research and Clinical Perspectives.* Arlington, VA: American Psychiatric Publishing.

Kirmayer, Laurence, and Allan Young. 1998. "Culture and Somatization: Clinical, Epidemiological, and Ethnographic Perspectives." *Psychosomatic Medicine* 60 (4): 420–30. http://dx.doi.org/10.1097/00006842-199807000-00006.

Kirmayer, Laurence J., and Duncan Pederson. 2014. "Toward a New Architecture for Global Mental Health." *Transcultural Psychiatry* 51 (6): 759–76.

Kitanaka, Junko. 2011. *Depression in Japan: Psychiatric Cures for a Society in Distress.* Princeton, NJ: Princeton University Press.

Kleinman, Arthur. 2014. "How We Endure." *Lancet* 383 (9912): 119–20. http://dx.doi.org/10.1016/S0140-6736(14)60012-X.

Kleinman, Arthur. 1995. *Writing at the Margin: Discourse between Anthropology and Medicine.* Berkeley: University of California Press.

Kleinman, Arthur. 1988a. *The Illness Narratives: Suffering, Healing and the Human Condition.* New York: Basic Books.

Kleinman, Arthur. 1988b. *Rethinking Psychiatry: From Cultural Category to Personal Experience.* New York: The Free Press.

Kleinman, Arthur. 1986. *Social Origins of Distress and Disease.* New Haven, CT: Yale University Press.

Kleinman, Arthur. 1980. *Patients and Healers in the Context of Culture: An Exploration of the Borderland between Anthropology, Medicine and Psychiatry.* Berkeley: University of California Press.

Kleinman, Arthur. 1977. "Depression, Somatization and the 'New Cross-Cultural Psychiatry.'" *Social Science & Medicine* 11 (1): 3–9. http://dx.doi.org/10.1016/0037-7856(77)90138-X.

Kleinman, Arthur, Veena Das, and Margaret Lock. 1996. "Introduction: Social Suffering." *Daedalus* 125: xi–xx.

Kleinman, Arthur, and Joan Kleinman. 1991. "Suffering and Its Professional Transformation: Toward an Ethnography of Interpersonal Experience." *Culture, Medicine and Psychiatry* 15 (3): 275–301. http://dx.doi.org/10.1007/BF00046540.

Kohrt, Brandon, and Emily Mendenhall, eds. 2015. *Global Mental Health: Anthropological Perspectives.* Walnut Creek, CA: Left Coast Press.

Kohrt, Brandon, Andrew Rasmussen, Bonnie Kaiser, Emily Haroz, Sujen Maharjan, Byamah Mutamba, Joop de Jong, and Devon Hinton. 2013. "Cultural Concepts of Distress and Psychiatric Disorders: Literature Review and Research Recommendations for Global Mental Health Epidemiology." *International Journal of Epidemiology* 43 (2): 365–406. http://dx.doi.org/10.1093/ije/dyt227.

Kraepelin, Emil. [1904] 2000. "Comparative Psychiatry." In *Cultural Psychiatry and Medical Anthropology. An Introduction and Reader,* edited by Simon Dein and Roland Littlewood, 38–42. London: The Athlone Press.

Kraepelin, Emil. [1893] 1990. "Psychiatrie." In *Psychiatry: A Textbook for Students and Physicians,* edited by Jacques Quen, and translated by Helga Metoui and Sabine Ayed. Canton, MA: Science History Publications.

Kraus, Rebecca. 2010. "Book Review of Didier Fassin and Richard Rechtman. Translated by Rachel Gomme. *The Empire of Trauma: An Inquiry into the Condition of Victimhood." Anthropological Quarterly* 83: 205–08.

Kugelman, Robert. 2009. "The Irritable Heart Syndrome in the American Civil War." In *Culture and Panic Disorder*, edited by Devon Hinton and Byron Good, 85–112. Stanford, CA: Stanford University Press.

Laing, R.D. 1964. *Sanity, Madness and the Family*. London: Penguin.

Lancet Global Mental Health Group. 2007. "Scale Up Services for Mental Disorders: A Call for Action." *Lancet* 370: 87–98.

Lassalle, Yvonne, and Maureen O'Dougherty. 1997. "In Search of Weeping Worlds: Economies of Agency and Politics of Representation in the Ethnography of Inequality." *Radical History Review* 69: 243–60.

Lawlor, Clark. 2012. *From Melancholia to Prozac: A History of Depression*. Oxford: Oxford University Press.

Leader, Darian. 2013. *Strictly Bipolar*. London: Penguin.

Leader, Darian. 2011. *What Is Madness?* London: Penguin.

Leavey, Gerard. 2010. "The Appreciation of the Spiritual in Mental Illness: A Qualitative Study of Beliefs among Clergy in the UK." *Transcultural Psychiatry* 47 (4): 571–90. http://dx.doi.org/10.1177/1363461510383200.

Lee, Boon-Ooi, Laurence Kirmayer, and Danielle Groleau. 2010. "Therapeutic Processes and Perceived Helpfulness of *Dang-Ki* (Chinese Shamanism) from the Symbolic Healing Perspective." *Culture, Medicine and Psychiatry* 34 (1): 56–105. http://dx.doi.org/10.1007/s11013-009-9161-3.

Lemelson, Robert. Dir. 2011. *Memory of My Face*. Afflictions: Culture and Mental Illness in Indonesia. Anthropology and Psychiatry Film Series. Watertown, MA: Documentary Educational Resources.

Lemelson, Robert. Dir. 2010a. *Bird Dancer*. Afflictions: Culture and Mental Illness in Indonesia. Anthropology and Psychiatry Film Series. Watertown, MA: Documentary Educational Resources.

Lemelson, Robert. Dir. 2010b. *Shadows and Illuminations*. Afflictions: Culture and Mental Illness in Indonesia. Anthropology and Psychiatry Film Series. Watertown, MA: Documentary Educational Resources.

Lende, Daniel H., and Greg Downey. 2012. "Neuroanthropology and the Encultured Brain." In *The Encultured Brain: An Introduction to Neuroanthropology*, edited by Daniel H. Lende and Greg Downey, 23–66. Cambridge, MA: MIT Press.

Leonhard, Karl. 1957. "Pathogenesis of Manic Depressive Disease." *Der Nervenarzt* 28: 271–72.

Lester, Rebecca. 2013a. "Lessons from the Borderline. Anthropology, Psychiatry and the Risks of Being Human." *Feminism & Psychology* 23 (1): 70–77. http://dx.doi.org/10.1177/0959353512467969.

Lester, Rebecca. 2013b. "Back from the Edge of Existence. A Critical Anthropology of Trauma." *Transcultural Psychiatry* 50 (5): 753–62. http://dx.doi.org/10.1177/1363461513504520.

Lévi-Strauss, Claude. 1963. *Structural Anthropology*. New York: Basic Books.

Lévi-Strauss, Claude. [1955] 1992. *Tristes Tropiques*. Translated by Doreen Weightman and John Weightman. London: Penguin. Originally published in 1955 by Librairie Plon.

Lewis-Fernández, Roberto, Neil Aggarwal, Sofie Bäärnhielm, Hans Rohlof, Laurence Kirmayer, Mitchell Weiss, Sushrut Jadhav, Ladson Hinton, et al. 2014. "Culture and Psychiatric Evaluation: Operationalizing Cultural Formulation for DSM-5." *Psychiatry* 77 (2): 130–54. http://dx.doi.org/10.1521/psyc.2014.77.2.130.

Lewis-Fernández, Roberto, Peter Guarnaccia, Igda Martinez, Ester Salman, Andrew Schmidt, and Michael Liebowitz. 2002. "Comparative Phenomenology of *Ataques de Nervios*, Panic Attacks, and Panic Disorder." *Culture, Medicine and Psychiatry* 26 (2): 199–223. http://dx.doi.org/10.1023/A:1016349624867.

Lidz, Theodore, Stephen Fleck, and Alice Cornelison. 1965. *Schizophrenia and the Family*. New York: International Universities Press.

Lin, Keh-Ming, Arthur Kleinman, and Tsung-Yi Lin. 1980. "Overview of Mental Disorders in Chinese Cultures: Overview of Clinical and Epidemiological Studies." In *Normal and Abnormal Behavior in Chinese Culture*, edited by Arthur Kleinman and Tsung-Yi Lin, 237–72. New York: Springer.

Littlewood, Roland. 2009. "How Universal Is Something We Can Call 'Therapy'? Some Implications of Non-Western Healing Systems for Intercultural Work." *Journal of Interprofessional Care* 5: 49–65.

Littlewood, Roland. 2002. *Pathologies of the West. An Anthropology of Mental Illness in Europe and America*. Ithaca, NY: Cornell University Press.

Lock, Margaret. 1993. *Encounters with Aging: Mythologies of Menopause in Japan and North America*. Berkeley: University of California Press.

Lovell, Anne, Stefania Pandolfo, Veena Das, and Sandra Laugier. 2013. *Face aux Désastres: une conversation à auatre voix sur la folie, le care et les grandes détresses collectives*. Paris: Les Editions d'Ithaque.

Luhrmann, Tanya. 2013. "Making God Real and Making God Good: Some Mechanisms through which Prayer May Contribute to Healing." *Transcultural Psychiatry* 50: 707–25.

Luhrmann, Tanya. 2012a. *When God Talks Back*. New York: Knopf.

Luhrmann, Tanya. 2012b. Living with Voices. *The American Scholar* (Summer). Available at: www.http://theamericanscholar.org/living-with-voices/#.VELpx8tozUA (accessed 7 July 2014).

Luhrmann, Tanya. 2010. "The Protest Psychosis: How Schizophrenia Became a Black Disease." *American Journal of Psychiatry* 167: 478–80.

Luhrmann, Tanya. 2007. "Social Defeat and the Culture of Chronicity: Or, Why Schizophrenia Does So Well Over There and So Badly Here." *Culture, Medicine and Psychiatry* 31 (2): 135–72. http://dx.doi.org/10.1007/s11013-007-9049-z.

Luhrmann, Tanya. 2001. *Of Two Minds*. New York: Vintage Books.

Luhrmann, Tanya, R. Padmavati, Hema Tharoor, and Akwasi Osei. 2015. "Hearing Voices in Different Cultures. A Social Kindling Hypothesis." *Topics in Cognitive Science* 7 (4): 646–63.

Malabou, Catherine. 2012. *The New Wounded: From Neurosis to Brain Damage*. Translated by Steven Miller. New York: Fordham University Press.

Manderson, Lenore, and Carolyn Smith-Morris, eds. 2010. *Chronic Conditions, Fluid States: Chronicity and the Anthropology of Illness*. New Brunswick, NJ: Rutgers University Press.

Martin, Emily. 2007. *Bipolar Expeditions: Mania and Depression in American Culture*. Princeton, NJ: Princeton University Press.

McCulloch, Jock. 2006. *Colonial Psychiatry and "The African Mind."* Cambridge: Cambridge University Press.

115

McLean, Athena. 2000. "From Ex-Patient Alternatives to Consumer Options: Consequences of Consumerism for Psychiatric Consumers and the Ex-Patient Movement." *International Journal of Health Services* 30 (4): 821–47. http://dx.doi.org/10.2190/3TYX-VRRK-XKHA-VB1Q.

Mehta, Vandana, Abishek De, and Chandrashekar Balachandran. 2009. "*Dhat* Syndrome: A Reappraisal." *Indian Journal of Dermatology* 54 (1): 89–90. http://dx.doi.org/10.4103/0019-5154.49002.

Metzl, Jonathan M. 2012. "Structural Competency." *American Quarterly* 64 (2): 213–18. http://dx.doi.org/10.1353/aq.2012.0017.

Metzl, Jonathan. 2010. *The Protest Psychosis*. Boston: Beacon Press.

Meyers, Todd. 2014. "Anesthesia." Somatosphere. Available at: http://somatosphere.net/2014/04/anesthesia.html (accessed 6 May 2014).

Meyers, Todd. 2013. *The Clinic and Elsewhere*. Seattle: University of Washington Press.

Miller, Kenneth, and Andrew Rasmussen. 2010. "War Exposure, Daily Stressors, and Mental Health in Conflict and Post-Conflict Settings: Bridging the Divide between Trauma-Focused and Psychosocial Frameworks." *Social Science & Medicine* 70 (1): 7–16. http://dx.doi.org/10.1016/j.socscimed.2009.09.029.

Mills, China. 2014. "Psychotropic Childhoods: Global Mental Health and Pharmaceutical Children." *Children & Society* 28 (3): 194–204. http://dx.doi.org/10.1111/chso.12062.

Mills, China. 2013. *Decolonizing Global Mental Health: The Psychiatrization of the Majority World*. New York: Routledge.

Mitchell, Juliet. 1974. *Psychoanalysis and Feminism*. New York: Basic Books.

Moncrieff, Joanna, D. Cohen, and John Mason. 2009. "The Subjective Experience of Taking Antipsychotic Drugs." *Acta Psychiatrica Scandinavia* 120: 102–11.

Moore, Henrietta. 2007. *The Subject of Anthropology: Gender, Symbolism and Psychoanalysis*. Oxford: Polity Press.

Myers, Neely Laurenzo. 2015. *Recovery's Edge: An Ethnography of Mental Health Care and Moral Agency*. Nashville: Vanderbilt University Press.

Nakamura, Karen. 2013. *A Disability of the Soul: An Ethnography of Schizophrenia and Mental Illness in Japan*. Ithaca, NY: Cornell University Press.

National Institute of Mental Health. 2010. "Grand Challenges in Global Mental Health." http://grandchallengesgmh.nimh.nih.gov/about.shtml (accessed 22 June 2016).

Nations, Marilyn. 2013. "Dead-Baby Dreams, Transfiguration and Recovery from Infant Death Trauma in Northeast Brazil." *Transcultural Psychiatry* 50 (5): 662–82. http://dx.doi.org/10.1177/1363461513497501.

Nations, Marilyn. 2009. *C'orte a Mortalha: o Callculo Humano da Morte Infantil no C'eara*. Rio de Janeiro: Fiocruz.

Nations, Marilyn. 2008. "Infant Death and Interpretive Violence in Northeast Brazil: Taking Bereaved C'earense Mothers' Narratives to Heart." *Cadernos de Saude Publica* 24 (10): 2239–48. http://dx.doi.org/10.1590/S0102-311X2008001000005.

Nichter, Mark. 2010. "Idioms of Distress Revisited." *Culture, Medicine and Psychiatry* 34 (2): 401–16. http://dx.doi.org/10.1007/s11013-010-9179-6.

Nichter, Mark. 1980. "The Layperson's Perception of Medicine as Perspective into the Utilization of Multiple Therapy Systems in the Indian Context." *Social Science and Medicine* 14: 225–33.

Nutt, David. 2014. "A Brave New World for Psychology." *Psychologist* 27: 658–61.

Obeyesekere, Gananath. 1990. *The Work of Culture. Symbolic Transformation in Psychoanalysis and Anthropology.* Chicago: University of Chicago Press.

Obeyesekere, Gananath. 1985. "Depression, Buddhism and the Work of Culture in Sri Lanka." In *Culture and Depression*, edited by Arthur Kleinman and Byron Good, 134–52. Berkeley: University of California Press.

Ong, Walter. 1987. "The Writer's Audience Is Always a Fiction." In *Twentieth Century Literary Theory*, edited by Vassilis Lambropoulos and David N. Miller, 401–22. Albany: State University of New York Press.

Pandolfo, Stefania. 2008. "The Knot of the Soul. Postcolonial Conundrums, Madness and the Imagination." In *Postcolonial Disorders*, edited by Mary-Jo DelVecchio Good, Sarah Hyde, Sarah Pinto, and Byron Good, 329–58. Berkeley: University of California Press. http://dx.doi.org/10.1525/california/9780520252233.003.0013.

Paris, Joel, and Hallie Zweig-Frank. 2001. "A 27-Year Follow-up of Patients with Borderline Personality Disorder." *Comprehensive Psychiatry* 42 (6): 482–87. http://dx.doi.org/10.1053/comp.2001.26271.

Parish, Steven. 2008. *Subjectivity and Suffering in American Culture. Possible Selves.* New York: Palgrave Macmillan. http://dx.doi.org/10.1057/9780230613188.

Parle, Julie. 2007. *States of Mind. Searching for Mental Health in Natal and Zululand, 1868–1918.* Scottsville, South Africa: University of KwaZulu-Natal Press.

Parnas, Josef, and Shaun Gallagher. 2015. "Phenomenology and the Interpretation of Psycho-Pathological Experience." In *Re-Visioning Psychiatry. Integrating Biological, Clinical and Cultural Perspectives*, edited by Laurence Kirmayer, Robert Lemelson, and Constance Cummings, 65–80. Cambridge: Cambridge University Press.

Patai, Raphael. [1973] 2002. *The Arab Mind.* Hobart: Hatherleigh Press.

Patel, Vikram. 2003. *Where There Is No Psychiatrist: A Mental Health Care Manual.* Glasgow: Bell and Bain.

Patel, Vikram, Gary S. Belkin, Arun Chockalingam, Janice Cooper, Shekhar Saxena, and Jürgen Unützer. 2013. "Grand Challenges: Integrating Mental Health Services into Priority Health Care Platforms." *PLoS Medicine* 10 (5): e1001448. http://dx.doi.org/10.1371/journal.pmed.1001448.

Patel, Vikram, Niall Boyce, Pamela Collins, Shekhar Saxena, and Richard Horton. 2011. "A Renewed Agenda for Global Mental Health." *Lancet* 378 (9801): 1441–42. http://dx.doi.org/10.1016/S0140-6736(11)61385-8.

Patel, Vikram, and Arthur Kleinman. 2003. "Poverty and Common Mental Disorders in Developing Countries." *Bulletin of the World Health Organization* (81) 8: 609–15.

Paul, Robert. 1989. "Psychoanalytic Anthropology." *Annual Review of Anthropology* 18 (1): 177–202. http://dx.doi.org/10.1146/annurev.an.18.100189.001141.

Peled, Micha. Dir. 2011. *Bitter Seeds.* San Francisco: Teddy Bear Films.

Pentecost, Michelle. 2016. "Introduction: The First Thousand Days of Life." Somatosphere. Available at: http://somatosphere.net/2016/04/introduction-the-first-thousand-days-of-life.html (accessed 11 April 2016).

Perris, Carlo. 1966. "A Study of Bipolar (Manic-Depressive) and Unipolar Recurrent Depressive Psychoses. Introduction." *Acta Psychiatrica Scandinavica* 194 (Supplementum): 9–14. http://dx.doi.org/10.1111/j.1600-0447.1966.tb11009.x.

Perspectives Group. 2009. *Harvesting Despair: Agrarian Crisis in India.* New Delhi: Perspectives Group.

Plath, Sylvia. 1963. *The Bell Jar.* London: Faber and Faber.

Poewe, Karla. 1996. "Writing Culture and Writing Fieldwork: The Proliferation of Experimental and Experiential Ethnographies." *Ethnos* 61 (3-4): 177–206. http://dx.doi.org/10.1080/00141844.1996.9981535.

Popovsky, Rabbi Mark A. 2010. "Special Issues in the Care of Ultra-Orthodox Jewish Psychiatric In-Patients." *Transcultural Psychiatry* 47 (4):647–72. http://dx.doi.org/10.1177/1363461510383747.

Potamianou, Anna. 1997. *Hope: A Shield in the Economy of Borderline States.* Oxon, NY: Routledge.

Rabinow, Paul. 2007. *Marking Time: On the Anthropology of the Contemporary.* Princeton, NJ: Princeton University Press.

Rahimi, Sadeq. 2015. *Meaning, Madness and Political Subjectivity: A Study of Schizophrenia and Culture in Turkey.* Oxon, NY: Routledge.

Raikhel, Eugene, and William Garriott, eds. 2013. *Addiction Trajectories.* Durham, NC: Duke University Press.

Rehbun, Linda, A. 1994. "A Heart Too Full: The Weight of Love in Northeast Brazil." *Journal of American Folklore* 104: 167–80.

Robbins, Joel. 2013. "Beyond the Suffering Subject: Toward an Anthropology of the Good." *Journal of the Royal Anthropological Institute* 19: 447–62. http://dx.doi.org/10.1111/1467-9655.12044.

Robbins, Richard. Dir. 2007. *Operation Homecoming: Writing the Wartime Experience.* London: The Documentary Group.

Rodrigues, Isabel Feo. 2006. "Book Review of João Biehl. Vita. Life in a Zone of Social Abandonment." *Anthropological Quarterly* 79: 773–76. http://dx.doi.org/10.1353/anq.2006.0053.

Rosaldo, Renato. 2014. *The Day of Shelly's Death: The Poetry and Ethnography of Grief.* Durham, NC: Duke University Press.

Rosaldo, Renato. 1980. *Ilongot Headhunting, 1883–1974: A Study in Society and History.* Stanford, CA: Stanford University Press.

Sahlins, Marshall, Thomas Bargatzky, Nurit Bird-David, John Clammer, Jacques Hamel, Keiji Maegawa, and Jukka Siikala. 1996. "The Sadness of Sweetness. The Native Anthropology of Western Cosmology." *Current Anthropology* 37 (3): 395–428. http://dx.doi.org/10.1086/204503.

Said, Edward. 1993. *Culture and Imperialism.* London: Chatto and Windus.

Said, Edward. 1978. *Orientalism.* London: Penguin.

Saks, Elyn. 2008. *The Center Cannot Hold: A Memoir of My Schizophrenia.* London: Virago.

Scarry, Elaine. 1985. *The Body in Pain: The Making and Unmaking of the World*. New York: Oxford University Press.

Scheper-Hughes, Nancy. 2008. "A Talent for Life: Reflections on Human Vulnerability and Resistance." *Ethnos* 73 (1): 25–56. http://dx.doi.org/10.1080/00141840801927525.

Scheper-Hughes, Nancy. 2001. *Saints, Scholars, and Schizophrenics: Mental Illness in Rural Ireland*. Berkeley: University of California Press.

Scheper-Hughes, Nancy. 1992. *Death Without Weeping: The Violence of Everyday Life in Brazil*. Berkeley: University of California Press.

Scheper-Hughes, Nancy. 1985. "Culture, Scarcity, and Maternal Thinking: Maternal Detachment and Infant Survival in a Brazilian Shantytown." *Ethos* 13 (4): 291–317. http://dx.doi.org/10.1525/eth.1985.13.4.02a00010.

Scheper-Hughes, Nancy. 1984. "Infant Mortality and Infant Care: Cultural and Economic Constraints on Nurturing in Northeast Brazil." *Social Science & Medicine* 19 (5): 535–46. http://dx.doi.org/10.1016/0277-9536(84)90049-2.

Schneider, Kurt. 1959. *Clinical Psychopathology*. New York: Grune and Stratton.

Schneider, Kurt. 1958. *Psychopathic Personalities*. London: Cassell Books.

Schneider, Kurt. 1920. "Die Schichtung des Emotionalen Lebens und der Aufbau der Depressionszustände." *Zeitschrift für die Gesamte Neurologie und Psychiatrie* 59 (1): 281–286. http://dx.doi.org/10.1007/BF02901090.

Schüll, Natasha Dow. 2012. *Addiction by Design: Machine Gambling in Las Vegas*. Princeton, NJ: Princeton University Press.

Seigel, Jerrold. 1994. "The Subjectivity of Structure: Individuality and Its Contradictions." In *Rediscovering History. Culture, Politics and the Psyche*, edited by Michael Roth, 349–70. Stanford: Stanford University Press.

Sessa, Ben. 2012. *The Psychedelic Renaissance: Reassessing the Role of Psychedelic Drugs in 21st-Century Psychiatry and Society*. London: Muswell Hill Press.

Shaw, Claire, and Lucy Ward. 2014. "Dark Thoughts: Why Mental Illness Is on the Rise in Academia." *The Guardian*, 6 March.

Shweder, Richard. 1988. "Suffering in Style." *Culture, Medicine and Psychiatry* 12 (4): 479–97. http://dx.doi.org/10.1007/BF00054499.

Sigaud, Lygia. 1995. "Fome'e Comportamentos Sociais: Problemas de Explicacao em Antropologia." *Mana* 1: 167–75.

Simmel, Georg. [1903] 2002. "The Metropolis and Mental Life." In *The Blackwell City Reader*, edited by Gary Bridge and Sophie Watson, 11–19. Oxford: Wiley-Blackwell.

Simons, Ronald C. 1996. *Boo! Culture, Experience, and the Startle Reflex*. New York: Oxford University Press.

Simons, Ronald C. 1983. "Latah II—Problems with a Purely Symbolic Interpretation. A Reply to Michael Kenny." *Journal of Nervous and Mental Disease* 171 (3): 168–75. http://dx.doi.org/10.1097/00005053-198303000-00006.

Simons, Ronald C. 1980. "The Resolution of the Latah Paradox." *Journal of Nervous and Mental Disease* 168 (4): 195–206. http://dx.doi.org/10.1097/00005053-198004000-00001.

Sinclair, Alex. 1957. *Field and Clinical Survey Report of the Mental Health of the Indigenes of the Territory of Papua and New Guinea*. Port Moresby: Government Printer.

Slaby, Jan, and Suparna Choudhury. 2011. "Proposal for a Critical Neuroscience." In *Critical Neuroscience*, edited by Suparna Choudhury and Jan Slaby, 27–51. Oxford: Wiley-Blackwell. http://dx.doi.org/10.1002/9781444343359.ch1.

Sorsdahl, Katherine, Dan Stein, and Alan Flisher. 2010. "Traditional Healer Attitudes and Beliefs Regarding Referral of the Mentally Ill to Western Doctors in South Africa." *Transcultural Psychiatry* 47 (4): 591–609. http://dx.doi.org/10.1177/1363461510383330.

Spencer, Jonathon. 1989. "Anthropology as a Kind of Writing." *Man* 24 (1): 145–65. http://dx.doi.org/10.2307/2802551.

Spivak, Gayatri Chakravorty. 1988. "Can the Subaltern Speak?" *Marxism and the Interpretation of Culture* 271–313. http://dx.doi.org/10.1007/978-1-349-19059-1_20.

Stotz-Ingenlath, Gabriele. 2000. "Epistemological Aspects of Eugen Bleuler's Conception of Schizophrenia in 1911." *Medicine, Health Care, and Philosophy* 3 (2): 153–59. http://dx.doi.org/10.1023/A:1009919309015.

Street, Brian, and Linda Thompson. 1993. "Culture Is a Verb: Anthropological Aspects of Language and Cultural Process." In *Language and Culture*, edited by David Graddol and Mike Byram, 23–43. Clevedon: BAAL in association with Multilingual Matters.

Summerfield, Derek. 2012. "Afterword: Against 'Global Mental Health.'" *Transcultural Psychiatry* 49 (3-4): 519–30. http://dx.doi.org/10.1177/1363461512454701.

Summerfield, Derek. 2008. "How Scientifically Valid Is the Knowledge Base of Global Mental Health?" *British Medical Journal* 336 (7651): 992–94. http://dx.doi.org/10.1136/bmj.39513.441030.AD.

Summerson Carr, E. 2011. *Scripting Addiction: The Politics of Therapeutic Talk and American Sobriety*. Princeton, NJ: Princeton University Press.

Suzuki, Katsuaki, Nori Takei, Matsayashi Kawai, Yoshio Minabe, and Norio Mori. 2003. "Is *Tajin Kyofusho* a Culture-Bound Syndrome?" *American Journal of Psychiatry* 160 (7): 1358. http://dx.doi.org/10.1176/appi.ajp.160.7.1358.

Szasz, Thomas. 1979. *Schizophrenia: The Sacred Symbol of Psychiatry*. Oxford: Oxford University Press.

Tajan, Nicolas. 2013. "Commonalities and Differences between Socially Withdrawn Young Adults (*hikikomori*) in France and Japan." *L'Évolution Psychiatrique* 78: 249–66.

Taylor, Barbara. 2014. *The Last Asylum: A Memoir of Madness in Our Times*. London: Hamish Hamilton.

Throop, Jason. 2010. *Suffering and Sentiment: Exploring the Vicissitudes of Pain and Experience in Yap*. Berkeley: University of California Press.

Timimi, Sami. 2008. "Child Psychiatry and Its Relationship to the Pharmaceutical Industry: Theoretical and Practical Issues." *Advances in Psychiatric Treatment* 14 (1): 3–9. http://dx.doi.org/10.1192/apt.bp.105.000901.

Tribe, Rachel. 2007 "Health Pluralism: A More Appropriate Alternative to Western Models of Therapy in the Context of the Civil Conflict and Natural Disaster in Sri Lanka?" *Journal of Refugee Studies* 20 (1): 21–36.

Tucker, Annie, and Robert Lemelson. 2011. *Memory of My Face: Film Guide*. http://www.der.org/resources/study-guides/memory-of-my-face-guide.pdf (accessed 21 June 2016).

United Nations Millennium Development Goals and Beyond. 2015. http://www.
un.org/millenniumgoals/ (accessed 5 September 2014).

Vaughan, Megan. 1991. *Curing Their Ills: Colonial Power and African Illness*. London:
Polity Press.

Wagner, Roy. 1975. *The Invention of Culture*. Chicago: University of Chicago Press.

Wakefield, Jerome. 2007. "The Concept of Mental Disorder: Diagnostic Implications
of the Harmful Dysfunction Analysis." *World Psychiatry* 6 (3): 149–56.

Waldram, James. 2014. "Healing History? Aboriginal Healing, Historical Trauma,
and Personal Responsibility." *Transcultural Psychiatry* 51 (3): 370–86. http://dx.doi.
org/10.1177/1363461513487671.

Waldram, James. 2012. *Hound Pound Narrative: Sexual Offender Habilitation and the
Anthropology of Therapeutic Intervention*. Berkeley: University of California Press.

Watters, Ethan. 2011. *Crazy Like Us: The Globalization of the American Psyche*. New York:
Free Press.

Wen-Shing, Tseng, and Jon Strelzer. 2013. *Culture and Psychopathology: A Guide to
Clinical Assessment*. New York: Routledge.

Whitaker, Robert. 2003. *Mad in America: Bad Science, Bad Medicine, and the Enduring
Mistreatment of the Mentally Ill*. New York: Perseus Publications.

Wilkinson, Iain, and Arthur Kleinman. 2016. *A Passion for Society: How We Think about
Human Suffering*. Berkeley: University of California Press.

Williamson, Thomas. 2010. "Researching Amok in Malaysia." In *Crossing Colonial
Historiographies: Histories of Colonial and Indigenous Medicines in Transnational
Perspective*, edited by Anne Digby, Waltraud Ernst, and Projit Mukarji, 37–56.
Newcastle-upon-Tyne: Cambridge Scholars Publishing.

World Health Organization (WHO). 2010. *International Statistical Classification of
Diseases and Related Health Problems, Tenth Revision* (ICD-10). Geneva: WHO.

World Health Organization (WHO). 2008. *mhGAP Mental Health Gap Action Programme.
Scaling Up Care for Mental, Neurological, and Substance Use Disorders*. Geneva: WHO.

World Health Organization (WHO). 2001a. *Mental Health. A Call for Action by
World Health Ministers*. http://www.who.int/mental_health/advocacy/en/Call_for_
Action_MoH_Intro.pdf (accessed 21 June 2016).

World Health Organization (WHO). 2001b. *World Health Report 2001: Mental Health:
New Understanding, New Hope*. Geneva: WHO.

Worthman, Carol, and Catherine Panter-Brick. 2008. "Homeless Street Children
in Nepal: Use of Allostatic Load to Assess the Burden of Childhood Adversity."
Development and Psychopathology 20 (1): 233–55. http://dx.doi.org/10.1017/
S0954579408000114.

Yap, Pow Meng. 1969. "The Culture-Bound Reactive Syndrome." In *Mental Health
Research in Asia and the Pacific*, edited by William Caudill and Tsung-yi Lin, 33–53.
Honolulu: East West Center Press.

Young, Allan. 2002. "The Self-Traumatized Perpetrator as a 'Transient Mental
Illness.'" *L'Évolution Psychiatrique* 67 (4): 630–50. http://dx.doi.org/10.1016/
S0014-3855(02)00162-7.

Young, Allan. 1995. *The Harmony of Illusions: Inventing Post-Traumatic Stress Disorder*.
Princeton, NJ: Princeton University Press.

INDEX

A

abandonment, 18

abnormality, and culture, 1–3

addiction, 19–20, 88–89, 90

adolescents, and pharmaceuticals, 82

Affliction (V. Das), 97

Afghans, hope and trauma, 50

Africans, colonialism and psychiatry, 28–29

Aggarwal, Neil, 34

"Algiers School" of colonial psychiatry, 28

Alma-Ata (Kazakhstan) conference and principles, 73

amok, 30, 31

anger, 36–37

anorexia nervosa, 36

anthropology and anthropologists

approaches to mental disorder, xx–xxi

contributions to mental disorder, 5–6, 95–97, 99–100

and culture, xxi, 3–6, 13

and culture-bound syndromes, 37–38

debates in and future directions, 98–100

and depression, 56–58

and DSM-5, xiv, 35–36

and globalization, 69

and global mental health, 67–68, 74–75

practical interventions, 98

and psychoanalysis, 76

and PTSD, 42, 50–51

and religion, 87

and schizophrenia, 9–10, 63

and trauma, 41, 49, 50

"Anthropology and the Abnormal" (Benedict), 1–2

Arabs, colonialism and psychiatry, 29

Aretxaga, Begoña, 75–76

Asad, Talal, on suffering, 21–22

asylums, and colonialism, 28

asylum seekers, and trauma, 46

ataque de nervios, 33–34, 35

auditory hallucinations. *See* voices affliction

Axis 1 and 2 type disorders, 11, 54–55

Ayu, Gusti, 91–92

B

Bäärnheilm, Sofie, 34

Bali (Indonesia), 53–54, 91–92

Barratt, Robert, on schizophrenia, 61

Bateson, Gregory, 7, 63

Benedict, Ruth, 1–3, 7

Bethel (Nakamura), 61

"Beyond the Suffering Subject" (Robbins), 15–16

Biehl, João, on suffering, 16–18

Big Pharma, 81–82

bioethnography, 5–6

biographies, as model for lived experience, 18–19

biology

and mental disorder, xvi–xx, 3–4, 5–6

and schizophrenia, 8–9, 11–12

bio-psychiatry and biomedicine, xvi

biosocial approaches, xix, 5–6

bipolar disorder, 55, 56, 58, 59–60

Bipolar Expeditions (Martin), 58–60

Bird Dancer (Lemelson), 91–92

Bitter Seeds (movie), 72

blacks, 8, 28–29

Bleuler, Eugen, and schizophrenia, 55

The Body in Pain: The Making and Unmaking of the World (Scarry), 20

borderline personality disorder (BPD), 37

Boyle, Mary, on schizophrenia, 8

brain, and trauma, 50

"brain disease-model," xvi

Brazil, 43, 44–45

Brodwin, Paul, 85

Bt cotton, 71–72

Bush Administration, reintegration of patients, 86

Buzzell, Colby, war and words, 91

C

Canguilhem, Georges, xviii
Carr, E. Summerson, on words and CBT, 90
Casa de locos (The Madhouse) (Goya), xviii
Catarina (Brazilian woman), and suffering, 16–18, 21
children, and global mental health, 71
China, 31, 57
chronicity, and suffering, 19–20
CIA, 73
cognitive-behavioral therapies (CBT), 90
colonialism
    and cultural psychiatry, 28–30
    and culture-bound syndromes, 30–32
    and global mental health, 73–75
    and postcolonial disorders, 75–77
colonial medicine, 73
comparative psychiatry, 28
Corin, Ellen, on schizophrenia, 62
Cornelison, Alice, 7
Csordas, Thomas, 18
cultural competency, xix–xx
cultural functionalism, 2
cultural psychiatry, xvii, 28–30
culture
    and abnormality, 1–3
    and anthropology, xxi, 3–6, 13
    and depression, 56–58
    and disorders in Western societies, 36–37
    and exoticism, 4–5
    and global mental health, 70
    in history, xviii–xix, 3–4
    and mental disorder, xvi–xx, 1–4, 5–6
    and nature, 5
    non-Western countries, 3–5
    as personality, 2
    and psychiatry, 10–12, 36–37
    and psychosis, 76
    and schizophrenia, 7–10, 60–62
    and sensation, 35
    and suffering, 15–16, 25
    and trauma, 42–44
Culture, Medicine, and Psychiatry, on proliferation of drugs, 82
Culture and Panic Disorder (Hinton and Good), 35–36
culture-bound syndromes
    and anthropologists, 37–38
    and colonialism, 30–32

and culture-free societies, 36–38
as culture-related phenomena, 32–34
definition, 30, 32
in DSM-5 and DSM-IV, 30, 31, 32–33, 34–35, 37
names and places of origin, 30, 35
and psychiatry, 29–32
and PTSD, 42–43
women and gender, 37
culture-free societies, 36–38

D

Das, Anindya, on farmers' suicides, 72
Das, Veena, 20–21, 49, 97, 98
Decolonizing Global Mental Health (Mills), 72
Dein, Simon, religion in mental disorder, 87
deinstitutionalization of patients, 85
De Lauri, Antonio, 24
DelVecchio Good, Mary-Jo, and colleagues, on postcolonial disorders, 75–76
dementia praecox, 54
dependent personality disorder, 36
depression and depressive disorders
    and anthropology, 56–58
    and culture, 56–58
    in DSM-5, 56, 57
    global mental health and local responses, 73
    theorization of, 55–56
    and work, 57–58
Descola, Philippe, 5
developed countries. *See* Western culture
developing countries, 3–5, 9–10
Devereux, George, xvii
dhat, 33
The Diagnostic and Statistical Manual of Mental Disorders (DSM-5)
    anger, 36–37
    Axis type disorders, 11
    bipolar disorder, 56
    borderline personality disorder (BPD), 37
    checklist for diagnosis, 11
    culture-bound syndromes, 30, 34–35, 37
    definitions in, xiii–xiv
    depression, 56, 57
    description, xiii–xiv
    mental disorder defined, xiv

South Africa, trauma in, 44
Southeast Asia, culture-bound
   syndromes, 31
Sri Lanka, depression in, 56–57
structural competency, xx
Subandi, Utami, on schizophrenia,
   61–62
suffering and "suffering subject"
   action on and responses to, 22–25
   critiques of, 24–25
   and culture, 15–16, 25
   and humanitarianism, 23–24
   and language, 17–19, 20, 21–22
   and the Other, 15–16
   social suffering, 15, 20–23, 24
   and time, 19–20
   writing of experiences, 18–19
"suffering slot anthropology," 15–16
"surplus health," 82
susto, 32

T
tajin kyosusho, 32
"A Talent for Life: Reflections on Human
   Vulnerability and Resistance"
   (Scheper-Hughes), 44
talking cures, 89–92
Tharoor, Hema, on schizophrenia, 60
"Theorizing the 'Subject' of Medical and
   Psychiatric Anthropology"
   (Good), xv
Throop, Jason, on suffering, 22
Tourette Syndrome, 91–92
trauma
   and anthropology, 41, 49, 50
   to brain, 50
   cross-cultural applicability, 44–46
   cultural variation and local responses,
      42–44
   definitions, 42
   and hope, 49–50
   and resilience, 44–45
   theories and alternatives to, 48–51
   in war and politics, 46–48
   See also post-traumatic stress disorder
      (PTSD)
Turkey, psychosis in, 76

U
United States
   anger, 36–37

bipolar disorder, 58–60
culture-related phenomena, 33–34
deinstitutionalization of patients, 85
psychiatry in, 11–12
recovery care and alternatives, 86–87
schizophrenia in, 8, 61
war healing and writing, 90–91

V
Vaughan, Megan, on cultural psychiatry,
   28–29
veterans, war healing and writing, 90–91
Vidarbha (India), farmers' suicides, 72
Vita (Biehl), 16–18
Vita (Brazil), 16–18
voices affliction, 53–54, 60, 63, 88

W
Wagner, Roy, on culture, 4
Wakefield, Jerome, social and scientific
   approaches, xvi
Waldram, James, on treatment
   programs, 85
war, 46–48, 90–91
Western culture
   and abnormality, 2
   cultural significance of disorders,
      36–37
   humanitarianism and suffering,
      23–24
   and schizophrenia, 9–10
   trauma in, 44
Whitaker, Robert, xxii
Wilkinson, Ian, on suffering, 22–23, 24
Williams, Robin, and bipolar
   disorder, 60
women, culture-bound syndromes, 37
words, and healing, 89–91
   See also language
work, 49, 57–58
World Health Organization (WHO)
   and global mental health, 68–69
   ICD-10, xiii, 30
   role and formation, 73
   and schizophrenia, 9, 10
writing, 18–19, 90–91
   See also literature

Y
Yap people, suffering in, 22
Young, Allan, on trauma, 44, 46, 47